# THE CULTURE
## OF RUSSIA

# SOCIETIES AND CULTURES
# RUSSIA

# THE CULTURE
# OF RUSSIA

EDITED BY EMILY SEBASTIAN

# Britannica®
### Educational Publishing

IN ASSOCIATION WITH

# ROSEN
EDUCATIONAL SERVICES

Published in 2019 by Britannica Educational Publishing (a trademark of Encyclopædia Britannica, Inc.) in association with The Rosen Publishing Group, Inc.
29 East 21st Street, New York, NY 10010

Distributed exclusively by Rosen Publishing.
To see additional Britannica Educational Publishing titles, go to rosenpublishing.com.

First Edition

**Britannica Educational Publishing**
J.E. Luebering: Executive Director, Core Editorial
Andrea R. Field: Managing Editor, Compton's by Britannica

**Rosen Publishing**
Amelie von Zumbusch: Editor
Nelson Sá: Art Director
Brian Garvey: Series Designer/Book Layout
Cindy Reiman: Photography Manager
Nicole Baker: Photo Researcher

**Library of Congress Cataloging-in-Publication Data**

Names: Sebastian, Emily, editor.
Title: The culture of Russia / edited by Emily Sebastian.
Description: New York : Britannica Educational Publishing, in Association with Rosen Educational Services, 2019. | Series: Societies and cultures : Russia |
Includes bibliographical references and index. | Audience: Grades 7–12.
Identifiers: LCCN 2017046382| ISBN 9781538301760 (library bound) | ISBN 9781538301777 (pbk.)
Subjects: LCSH: Russia (Federation)—Civilization—Juvenile literature. | Arts—Russia (Federation)—Juvenile literature. | Popular culture--Russia (Federation)—Juvenile literature.
Classification: LCC DK510.762 .C855 2017 | DDC 947—dc23
LC record available at https://lccn.loc.gov/2017046382

*Manufactured in the United States of America*

**Photo credits:** Cover, p. 3 Oleg Proskurin/Shutterstock.com; cover and interior pages (flag) fckncg/Shutterstock.com; cover and interior pages (emblem) N-sky/iStock/Thinkstock; p. 10 Richard Nowitz/National Geographic Image Collection/Getty Images; p. 15 Miles Ertman/robertharding/Getty Images; p. 18 Peter Turnley/Corbis Historical/Getty Images; p. 20 AFP/Getty Images; p. 22 finaeva i/Shutterstock.com; pp. 28-29 ©ID1974/Fotolia; pp. 32-33 Alexander Nemenov/AFP/Getty Images; pp. 34-35 Ted Thai/The LIFE Picture Collection/Getty Images; p. 39 ©Encyclopaedia Britannica, Inc.; p. 46 Boyd Norton; pp. 50-51 Andrey Nekrasov/age fotostock/Getty Images; pp. 56-57 df028/Shutterstock.com; p. 58 © Sovfoto; p. 62 © Courtesy of the Moscow Art Theatre Museum. Photograph, Sovfoto; p. 64 Vyacheslav Prokofyev/TASS/Getty Images; p. 66 swim ink 2 llc/Corbis Historical/Getty Images; p. 72 © Novosti Press Agency; p. 75 © Novosti/Sovfoto; p. 80 © Yale University Art Gallery. Gift of collection Société Anonyme (1941.553); p. 83 Imagno/Hulton Archive/Getty Images; p. 85 SVF2/Universal Images Group/Getty Images; p. 89 nikolpetr/Shutterstock.com; p. 94 Vladimir Sazonov/Shutterstock.com; p. 98 © Tatlin. Photograph © Moderna Museet, Stockholm; p. 101 Photos.com/JupiterImages; p. 105 Universal Images Group/Getty Images; p. 107 © From *Letters of Fyodor Michailovitch Dostoevsky to his Family and Friends* translated by Ethel Colburn Mayne, 1914; p. 110 © David Magarshack; p. 112 Heritage Images/Hulton Archive/Getty Images; p. 114 Steve Liss/The LIFE Images Collection/Getty Images.

# CONTENTS

# INTRODUCTION

**R**ussia's culture represents a melding of native Slavic traditions and influences from a variety of foreign cultures. Beginning in the 800s, following contact with Christian missionaries from the Byzantine Empire, the borrowings were primarily from Eastern Orthodox Byzantine culture. From the 1300s to the 1600s Asian influences brought by the Mongol occupiers were added to the cultural mix. Finally, since the 1700s, the cultural heritage of western Europe has contributed to modern Russian culture.

Russia has great diversity, with more than 120 distinct ethnic groups. Ethnic Russians make up about four-fifths of the population. The largest minority groups include the Tatars, Ukrainians, Bashkir, Chuvash, Chechen, Armenian, Mordvin, and Belarusian. The Eastern Orthodox branch of Christianity is the foremost religion in Russia. More than half of all Russians belong to the Russian Orthodox Church. Religious activities were restricted by the government during the Soviet years, but nationalists in the post-Soviet era closely tied Russian identity to the Orthodox faith. More than one third of the population identify as nonreligious or atheist. Muslims make up Russia's second largest religious group.

Because musical instruments were forbidden in Russian Orthodox church services, Russian music and consequently opera were delayed in development as an art form until more recent times. Since then Russian operas, symphonies, instrumental compositions, and art songs have flourished. Most are based on the melodic

and rhythmic patterns of Russian folk music and nationalistic themes.

Russian theatre originally was inspired by folk entertainment and later influenced by foreign models much like the ballet. At the end of the 19th century Konstantin Stanislavsky founded the Moscow Art Theater, where Russian theatre art came of age. Realistic plays produced there, among them the works of Chekhov and Gorky, stimulated the modern "method" school of acting.

Film developed during the period when Russia was part of the Soviet Union and was closely related to the propaganda efforts of the Communist regime. Such Soviet directors as Sergey Eisenstein, Vsevolod Pudovkin, Aleksandr Dovzhenko, and Lev Kuleshov produced film masterpieces inspired by revolutionary fervor. Russian cinema saw a gradual revitalization, however, under the new policy of *glasnost* ("openness") in the mid-1980s and the subsequent dissolution of communism.

Russian art was the servant of the Orthodox church until the reign of Peter I (also known as Peter the Great). Icon painting reached its zenith as a Russian art form in the 14th and 15th centuries. Modern Westernized painting and sculpture date from Peter's reforms after 1700. The stress on socialist realism in art as well as literature hampered artistic creativity beginning in the 1920s. Experimental art typically was banned and forced underground. With the opening of Soviet society in the 1980s, however, public exhibits of modern art were again permitted.

*One of the world's great museums, the Hermitage was founded in 1764 by Catherine the Great. Located in St. Petersburg, it initially served as a private gallery for the empress.*

Beginning in the 10th century Russian architecture was influenced by contacts with the Byzantine Empire. From the outset, however, Russian buildings had a higher, narrower silhouette than their Byzantine models. Russians experimented with the dome, which was derived from the yurt—a circular tent used by Central Asian nomads. This led to the onion-shaped domes characteristic of Russian Orthodox churches. Soviet buildings were pragmatic products of standardized architecture. Since the 1960s more innovative architectural styles have appeared.

The Russian literary tradition began with a body of proverbs, folktales, legends, and heroic ballads that passed orally among the earliest East Slavic tribes. Until the reign of Peter the Great in the late 17th and early 18th centuries, written literature was mainly religious in nature. The 1800s are recognized as the Golden Age of Russian literature, a time when it began to show a conscience, especially regarding serfdom and the downtrodden. Aleksandr Pushkin, often described as the "Russian Shakespeare," blended European and native Russian influences to reflect the thoughts, moods, and deeds of the society in which he lived. Other great writers of the Golden Age include Mikhail Lermontov, Nikolay Gogol, Ivan Goncharov, Ivan Turgenev, Fyodor Dostoyevsky, Leo Tolstoy, Anton Chekhov, Maksim Gorky, and Aleksandr Blok. Chekhov, Gorky, and Blok wrote works that overlapped the 19th and 20th centuries. With them came another literary and artistic revival, designated sometimes as the Silver Age. During the Soviet era, literature served the political regime. The collapse of the Soviet regime brought an end to government censorship and freed writers to engage in radical experimentalism.

# CHAPTER ONE

# THE ROOTS OF RUSSIAN CULTURE

Russia's unique and vibrant culture developed, as did the country itself, from a complicated interplay of native Slavic cultural material and borrowings from a wide variety of foreign cultures. In the Kievan period (c. 10th–13th century), the borrowings were primarily from Eastern Orthodox Byzantine culture. During the Muscovite period (c. 14th–17th century), the Slavic and Byzantine cultural substrates were enriched and modified by Asiatic influences carried by the Mongol hordes. Finally, in the modern period (since the 18th century), the cultural heritage of western Europe was added to the Russian melting pot.

## THE KIEVAN PERIOD

Although many traces of the Slavic culture that existed in the territories of Kievan Rus survived beyond its Christianization (which occurred, according to *The Russian Primary Chronicle*, in 988), the cultural system that organized the lives of the early Slavs is far from being understood. From the 10th century, however, enough material has survived to provide a reasonably accurate portrait of Old Russian cultural life. High culture in Kievan Rus was primarily ecclesiastical. Literacy was not widespread, and artistic composition was undertaken almost exclusively by monks. The earliest circulated literary works were translations from Greek into Old Church Slavonic (a South Slavic dialect that was, in this period, close enough to Old Russian to be understandable). By the 11th century, however, monks were producing original works (on Byzantine models), primarily hagiographies, historical chronicles, and homilies. At least one great secular work was produced as well: the epic *The Song of Igor's Campaign*, which dates from the late 12th century and describes a failed military expedition against the neighbouring Polovtsy. Evidence also exists (primarily in the form of church records of suppression) of a thriving popular culture based on pre-Christian traditions centring on harvest, marriage, birth, and death rituals.

The most important aspects of Kievan culture for the development of modern Russian culture, however, were not literary or folkloric but rather artistic and architectural. The early Slavic rulers expressed their religious piety and displayed their wealth through the construction of stone churches, at first in Byzantine style (such as the 11th-century Cathedral of St. Sophia, which still stands in Kiev, Ukraine) and later in a distinctive Russian style (best preserved today in churches in and around the city of Vladimir, east of Moscow). The interiors of many of these churches were ornately decorated with frescoes and icons.

# THE MUSCOVITE PERIOD

The Mongol (Tatar) invasions of the early 13th century decimated Kievan Rus. By the time Russian political and cultural life began to recover in the 14th century, a new centre had arisen: Muscovy (Moscow). Continuity with Kiev was provided by the Orthodox church, which had acted as a beacon of national life during the period of Tatar domination and continued to play the central role in Russian culture into the 17th century. As a result, Russian cultural development in the Muscovite period was quite different from that of western Europe, which at this time was experiencing the secularization of society and the rediscovery of the classical cultural heritage that characterized the Renaissance. At first the literary genres employed by Muscovite writers were the same as those that had dominated in Kiev. The most remarkable literary monuments of the Muscovite period, however, are unlike anything that came before. The correspondence between Tsar Ivan IV (Ivan the Terrible) and Andrey Mikhaylovich, Prince Kurbsky during the 1560s and '70s is particularly noteworthy. Kurbsky, a former general in Ivan's army, defected to Poland, whence he sent a letter critical of the tsar's regime. Ivan's diatribes in response are both wonderful expressions of outraged pride and literary tours de force that combine the highest style of

This church is known as the Cathedral of Vasily Blazhenny (St. Basil the Blessed) after Basil, the Russian holy fool who was buried in the church vaults.

Muscovite hagiographic writing with pithy and vulgar attacks on his enemy. Similarly vigorous in style is the first full-scale autobiography in Russian literature, Avvakum Petrovich's *The Life of the Archpriest Avvakum, by Himself* (c. 1672–75).

As in the Kievan period, however, the most significant cultural achievements of Muscovy were in the visual arts and architecture rather than in literature. Russian architects continued to design and build impressive churches, including the celebrated Cathedral of St. Basil the Blessed on Moscow's Red Square. Built to commemorate the Russian capture of Kazar, the Tatar capital, St. Basil's is a perfect example of the confluence of Byzantine and Asiatic cultural streams that characterizes Muscovite culture. The Moscow school of icon painting produced great masters, among them Dionisy and Andrey Rublyov (whose *Old Testament Trinity*, now in Moscow's Tretyakov Gallery, is among the most revered icons ever painted).

## THE EMERGENCE OF MODERN RUSSIAN CULTURE

The gradual turn of Russia toward western Europe that began in the 17th century led to an almost total reorientation of Russian interests during the reign of Peter I (1682–1725). Although Peter was not particularly interested in cultural questions, the influx of Western ideas (which accompanied the technology Peter found so attractive) and the weakening of the Orthodox church led to a cultural renaissance during the reigns of his successors. In the late 1730s poets Mikhail Lomonosov and Vasily Trediakovsky carried out reforms as far-reaching as those of Peter. Adapting German syllabotonic versification to Russian, they developed the system of "classical" metres that prevails in Russian poetry to this day. In the 1740s, in imitation of French Neoclassicism, Aleksandr Sumarokov wrote the first Russian stage tragedies. In the course of the century, Russian writers assimilated all the European genres; although much of their work was derivative, the comedies of Denis Fonvizin and the powerful, solemn odes of Gavrila Derzhavin were original and have remained part of the active Russian cultural heritage. Prose fiction made its appearance at the end of the century in the works of the sentimentalist Nikolay Karamzin. By the beginning of the 19th century, after a 75-year European cultural apprenticeship, Russia had developed a flexible secular literary language, had a command of modern Western literary forms, and was ready to produce fully original cultural work.

## SOCIAL CUSTOMS

During the Soviet era most customs and traditions of Russia's imperial past were suppressed, and life was strictly controlled and regulated by the state through its vast intelligence network. Beginning in the 1980s, Mikhail Gorbachev's reforms eased political and social restrictions, and common traditions and folkways, along with the open practice of religion, began to reappear.

Many folk holidays, which are often accompanied by traditional foods, have gained popularity and have become vital elements of popular culture. Festivities generally include street carnivals that feature entertainers and children in traditional Russian dress. Boys usually wear a long-sleeved red or blue shirt with a round, embroidered collar, while girls wear a three-piece ensemble consisting of a red or green *sarafan* (jumper), a long-sleeved peasant blouse, and an ornate *kokoshnik* (headdress).

Maslyanitsa, the oldest Russian folk holiday, marks the end of winter; a purely Russian holiday, it originated during pagan times. During Maslyanitsa ("butter"), pancakes—symbolizing the sun—are served with cav-

*These women are wearing the traditional Russian* sarafan *and* kokoshnik. *Both garments have a long history.*

iar, various fish, nuts, honey pies, and other garnishes and side dishes. The meal is accompanied by tea in the ever-present samovar (tea kettle) and is often washed down with vodka.

Baked goods are ubiquitous on Easter, including round-shaped sweet bread and Easter cake. Traditionally, *pashka*, a mixture of sweetened curds, butter, and raisins, is served with the cake. Hard-boiled eggs painted in bright colours also are staples of the Easter holiday.

The Red Hill holiday is observed on the first Sunday after Easter and is considered the best day for wedding ceremonies. In summer the Russian celebration of Ivan Kupalo (St. John the Baptist) centres on water, and celebrants commonly picnic or watch fireworks from riverbanks.

Another popular traditional holiday is the Troitsa (Pentecost), during which homes are adorned with fresh green branches. Girls often make garlands of birch branches and flowers to put into water for fortune-telling. In the last month of summer, there is a cluster of three folk holidays—known collectively as the Spas—that celebrate honey and the sowing of the apple and nut crops, respectively.

Russia also has several official holidays, including the Russian Orthodox Christmas (January 7), Victory Day in World War II (May 9), Independence Day (June 12), and Constitution Day (December 12). Women's Day (March 8), formerly known as International Women's Day and celebrated elsewhere in the world by its original name, was established by Soviet authorities to highlight the

advances women made under communist rule. During the holiday women usually receive gifts such as flowers and chocolates.

## DAILY LIFE

Although a wide array of imported packaged products are now found in Russian cities, traditional foods and ingredients remain popular, including cabbage, potatoes, carrots, sour cream, and apples—the principal ingredients of borsch, the famous Russian soup made with beets. Normally, Russians prefer to finish their daily meals with a cup of tea or coffee (the latter more common in the larger cities). Also popular is kvass, a traditional beverage that can be made at home from stale black bread. On a

# INTERNATIONAL WOMEN'S DAY

Around the world, March 8 has been set aside as International Women's Day (IWD), a holiday honouring the achievements of women and promoting women's rights. A national holiday in numerous countries, it has been sponsored by the United Nations (UN) since 1975.

International Women's Day (IWD) grew out of efforts in the early 20th century to promote women's rights, especially suffrage. In its campaign for female enfranchisement, the Socialist Party of America in 1909 held the first National Woman's Day. Encouraged by German activist Clara Zetkin, the International Socialist Congress agreed in 1910 to create an international version of the US holiday, and on March 19, 1911, the first IWD was held in Austria, Denmark, Germany, and Switzerland. More than one million people attended rallies marking the day. On March 8 (February 24 under the calendar in use at the time), 1917, women in Petrograd (St. Petersburg), Russia, marked the day by staging a strike to protest food shortages, poor living conditions, and World War I. This strike for "bread and peace" helped give rise to the Russian Revolution of 1917, which led to the abdication of Nicholas II on March 15 (March 2). In 1921 the date of the IWD was officially changed to March 8.

In the following decades, the success of the suffrage movement contributed to a decline in the popularity of the IWD. However, aided by the growth of feminism in the 1960s and UN sponsorship (1975), the IWD experienced a revitalization in the late 20th century. Today, it is an important occasion for promoting women's issues and rights, especially in developing countries.

hot summer day, chilled kvass is used to make *okroshka*, a traditional cold soup laced with cucumbers, boiled eggs, sausages, and salamis.

Vodka, the national drink of Russia, accompanies many family meals, especially on special occasions. The basic vodkas have no additional flavouring, but they are sometimes infused with cranberries, lemon peel, pepper, or herbs. Vodka is traditionally consumed straight and is chased by a fatty salt herring, a sour cucumber, a pickled mushroom, or a piece of rye bread with butter. It is considered bad manners and a sign of weak character to become visibly intoxicated from vodka.

*This bowl of borsch is served in a bowl painted in the* khokhloma *style. This traditional Russian folk art uses red, black, and gold and is heavily lacquered.*

The growth of the Russian middle class has generated dramatic changes in Russia's lifestyles and social customs. Travel abroad has become popular, and consumption, particularly of imported luxury goods, has increased. Many wealthy individuals have purchased private land and built second homes, often of two or three stories. Russia's middle class has adopted values that are distinctly different from Soviet practice. The new values include self-reliance and viewing work as source of joy and pride; the middle class also tends to avoid political extremes, to participate in charitable organizations, and to patronize theatres and restaurants. Estimates of the size of the middle class vary (as do definitions of it), but it is generally assumed that it constitutes about one-fourth of Russian society, and much of that is concentrated in Moscow, St. Petersburg, and other urban areas.

The rebirth of religion is another dimension of the changed lifestyles of new Russia. Although many Russians are nonbelievers, religious institutions have filled the vacuum created by the downfall of communist ideology, and even many nonbelievers participate in the now-ubiquitous religious festivities.

## HEALTH AND WELFARE

Public welfare funds from the state budget, enterprises, and trade unions are used substantially to improve the material and social conditions of workers in Russia. Social welfare programs formerly were funded by the central government, but in the 1990s employer-based social insurance and pension funds, to which workers also contributed, were introduced. A major portion of the public welfare budget funds free medical service, training, pensions, and scholarships. Russian workers and professionals receive paid vacations of up to one month.

During much of the Soviet period, advances in health care and material well-being led to a decline in mortality, the control or eradication of the more dangerous infectious diseases, and an increase in the average life span. After 1991, however, public health deteriorated dramatically.

In the 1990s the death rate reached its highest level of the 20th century (excluding wartime). Life expectancy fell dramatically (though it began to rise again by the end of the decade), and infectious diseases that had been under control spread again. In addition, the country suffered high rates of cancer, tuberculosis, and heart disease. Various social, ecological, and economic factors underlay these developments, including funding and medicine shortages, insufficiently paid and trained medical personnel (e.g., many medical schools lack sufficient supplies and instructors), poor intensive and emergency care, the limited development of specialized services such as maternity and hospice care, contaminated food and drinking water, duress caused by economic dislocation, poor nutrition, contact with toxic substances in the workplace, and high rates of alcohol and tobacco consumption. Air pollution in heavily industrialized areas has led to relatively high rates of lung cancer in these regions, and high incidences of stomach cancer have occurred in regions where consumption of carbohydrates is high and intake of fruits, vegetables, milk, and animal proteins is low.

Alcoholism, especially among men, has long been a severe public health problem in Russia. At the beginning of the 21st century, it was estimated that some one-third of men and one-sixth of women were addicted to alcohol. The problem is particularly acute in rural areas and among the Evenk, Sakha, Koryak, and Nenets in Russia's northern regions. Widespread alcoholism has its origins in the Soviet-era "vodka-based economy," which countered shortages in the supply of food and consumer goods with the production of vodka, a nonperishable product that was easily transportable. The government has sponsored media campaigns to promote healthy living and imposed strict tax regulations aimed at reducing the profitability of vodka producers; in addition, group-therapy sessions (e.g., Alcoholics Anonymous) have spread. There also have been proposals to prohibit the sale of hard liquors in the regions with the highest rates of alcoholism.

## EDUCATION

Education in the Soviet Union was highly centralized, with the state owning and operating nearly every school. The curriculum was rigid, and the system aimed to indoctrinate students in the communist system. As with many aspects of the Soviet system, schools were often forced to operate in crowded facilities and with limited resources.

With democratization there was widespread support for educational reforms. In 1992 the federal government passed legislation enabling regions where non-Russians predominated to exercise some degree of autonomy in education; still, diplomas can be conferred only in the Russian, Bashkir, and Tatar languages, and the federal government has responsibility for designing and distributing textbooks, licensing teachers, and setting the requirements for instruction in the Russian language, sciences, and mathematics. School finance and the humanities, history, and social science curricula are entrusted to regional authorities.

Preschool education in Russia is very well developed; some four-fifths of children aged three to six attend crèches (day nurseries) or kindergartens. Schooling is compulsory for nine years. It starts from age seven (in some areas from six) and leads to a basic general education certificate. An additional two or three years of schooling are required for the secondary-level certificate, and some seven-eighths of Russian students continue their education past this level. Non-Russian schoolchildren are taught in their own language, but Russian is a compulsory subject at the secondary level.

Admission to an institute of higher education is selective and highly competitive: first-degree courses usually take five years. Higher education is conducted almost entirely in Russian, although there are a few institutions, mainly in the minority republics, where the local language is also used.

Russia's oldest university is Moscow State University, which was founded in 1755. Throughout the 19th century and into the 20th, Russian universities in Moscow, St. Petersburg, and Kazan produced world-class scholars, notably the mathematician Nikolay Lobachevsky and the chemist Dmitry Mendeleyev. Although universities suffered severely during the purges of the Stalinist regime, a number have continued to provide high-quality education, particularly in the sciences. In addition to Moscow State University, the most important institutions include St. Petersburg State University (founded 1819) and Novosibirsk State University (1959).

Since the demise of the Soviet Union, the quantity and diversity of universities and institutes have undergone unprecedented expansion. In 1991 the country had some 500 institutions of higher education, all of which were controlled by the state. By the beginning of the 21st century, the number of state schools had increased by nearly one-fifth, though many suffered from inadequate state funding, dated equipment, and overcrowding. The state schools were joined by more than 300 private colleges and universities. which were all established after 1994. Licensed by the state, these schools generally enjoyed better funding than the state schools; however, they were very costly and served mainly Russia's new middle class.

## CULTURAL INSTITUTIONS

Some of the most-renowned museums in the world are located in Moscow and St. Petersburg. In Moscow the

Pushkin Fine Arts Museum houses treasures of western European art, while the Tretyakov Gallery has a strong collection of Russian art. Moscow's Kremlin, the former seat of communist power and the home of the Russian president, also contains a series of museums that include notable cathedrals and features the stunning architecture of the Kremlin building. The Tolstoy Museum Estate in Moscow features an excellent literary collection. In St. Petersburg the Hermitage is one of the great art museums of the world, the Russian Museum displays the world's largest collection of Russian art, and the Russian Museum of Ethnography details Russian culture and daily life throughout history. St. Petersburg is also home to the country's oldest museum, the Kunstkammer (formally Peter the Great's Museum of Anthropology

and Ethnography), which is now under the direction of the history department of the prestigious Russian Academy of Sciences. Moreover, in the suburbs of St. Petersburg, the former tsarist palaces at Pavlovsk, Pushkin, and

*This hall is in the Palace of Facets, one of several palaces inside the Kremlin. The palace was named for the exterior finish of faceted, white stone squares.*

Peterhof have been restored as museums. They are popular destinations for both Russians and foreign tourists.

Elsewhere, there also are various notable museums, many of which specialize in regional art, ethnography, and historical collections. For example, the Archangelsk State Museum, founded in 1737, houses collections that focus on the history of Russia's north coast, and the State United Museum of the Republic of Tatarstan has a wide array of decorative art and historical, archaeological, and ethnographic resources from Tatarstan. The Yaroslavl State Historical, Architectural, and Art Museum-Preserve offers an extensive collection focusing on Russian history and culture. Russian private philanthropy in the post-Soviet era resulted in the establishment of a number of important foundations to support the arts and education, including the Vladimir Potanin Foundation, the Open Russia Foundation, and the Dynasty Foundation.

## SPORTS AND RECREATION

Sports played a major role in the Soviet state in the post-World War II period. The achievements of Soviet athletes in the international arena, particularly in the Olympic Games (the Soviets first participated in the 1952 Summer and the 1956 Winter Olympics), were a source of great national pride. Although Soviet athletes were declared amateurs, they were well supported by the Sports State Committee. Soviet national teams were especially successful in ice hockey—winning numerous world championships and Olympic gold medals—volleyball, and, later, basketball. Soviet gymnasts and track and field athletes (male and female), weight lifters, wrestlers, and boxers were consistently among the best in the world. Even since the collapse of the Soviet empire, Russian athletes have continued to dominate international competition in these areas. In 2016 a massive state-sponsored doping operation was uncovered by international athletic officials, and Russia was banned from track and field events at the 2016 Summer Games in Rio de Janeiro. The International Paralympic Committee banned Russia from its 2016 games as well as the 2018 Winter Games in Pyeongchang, South Korea.

As in most of the world, football (soccer) enjoys wide popularity in Russia. At the centre of the country's proud tradition is legendary goalkeeper Lev Yashin, whose spectacular play in the 1956 Olympics helped Russia capture the gold medal. Today there are three professional divisions for men, and the sport is also growing in popularity among women. In 2010 Russia was chosen to host the 2018 World Cup finals.

In 2014, the Winter Olympics took place in the city of Sochi, along the coast of the Black Sea. The Sochi Games marked the first time that the Winter Olympics were held in Russia. The country had previously been home to the Olympics when Moscow hosted the 1980 Summer Games. Sochi was awash in controversy in the months leading up to the games, as the choice of a city with a temperate climate as a Winter Games site led to concerns about whether there would be adequate snow cover. Moreover, the construction of venues and other buildings ran far behind schedule, and preparations were plagued by allegations of mismanagement and corruption. Russia reportedly spent $51 billion on the games, a total that surpassed any paid by a previous host country. In addition, there were numerous security threats in the buildup to the games, as well as political unrest in nearby Ukraine, and the June 2013 passage of an antihomosexuality bill in the Russian parliament raised the possibility of protests derailing the Olympics. A mechanical failure during the opening ceremonies prevented one of the rings in a light display of the Olympic logo from deploying, which was seen as foreboding by many media members, but the

*As is often the case at the Olympics, the 2014 Sochi Games started with a lavish opening ceremony featuring a fireworks display.*

Sochi Olympics nevertheless progressed as smoothly as any other contemporary Winter Games.

Ice hockey was introduced to Russia only during the Soviet era, yet the national team soon dominated international competitions. The Soviet squad claimed more than 20 world championships between 1954 and 1991. The success of the national team can be attributed to both the Soviet player-development system and the leadership of coach Anatoly Tarasov, who created the innovative

team passing style characteristic of Soviet hockey. Goaltender Vladislav Tretiak (the first Soviet player inducted into the Hockey Hall of Fame in Toronto) and defenseman Vyacheslav Fetisov (who was among the first players whom Soviet authorities allowed to play in the North American National Hockey League [NHL]) were two of the finest players on those great Soviet teams. Although Russia's top professional league is quite popular, many of the best Russian players now ply their trade in the NHL.

Russia has had no peer on the international chess scene. The first Russian world chess champion was Alexander Alekhine, who left Russia after the revolution in 1917.

Undaunted by Alekhine's departure, the Soviet Union was able to produce top-ranked players by funding chess schools to find and train talented children. The best of these students were then supported by the state— they were the first chess professionals—at a time when no one in the West could make a living wage from chess alone. From 1948, Soviet and Russian grand masters, including Mikhail Botvinnik, Vasily Smyslov, Boris Spassky, Anatoly Karpov, Garry Kasparov, and Vladimir Kramnik, held the title of world champion almost continuously. During the same period, three Russian women reigned as women's world champion: Ludmilla Rudenko, Olga Rubtsova, and Elizaveta Bykova. Earlier, Vera Menchik-Stevenson, who became a British citizen in 1937, was world champion from 1927 until her death in 1944.

On the amateur level, the lack of facilities and equipment has prevented many average Russian citizens from participating in sporting activities, but jogging, football, and fishing are popular pastimes.

## MEDIA AND PUBLISHING

Russian 19th-century journalism was extremely vigorous, with newspapers and monthly "thick" journals being the most important forums. Daily newspapers and monthly journals of all political and artistic stripes con-

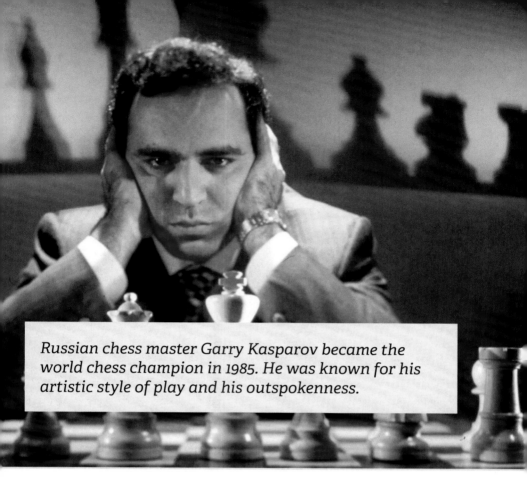

Russian chess master Garry Kasparov became the world chess champion in 1985. He was known for his artistic style of play and his outspokenness.

tinued to appear in the immediate aftermath of the 1917 revolution. However, the state's desire to control sources of information and propaganda manifested itself quickly, and most independent publications were eliminated by the early 1920s. What remained were the ubiquitous daily duo of *Pravda* ("Truth") and *Izvestiya* ("News"). Journals were in a somewhat better position, especially those that published mostly works of literature. Periodicals such as *Krasnaya nov* ("Red Virgin Soil") and *LEF* ("The Left Front of Art") published much significant literature in the 1920s. In the 1960s this tradition was revived by the journal *Novy mir* ("New World"), which in the 1980s was joined by a revitalized *Ogonyok* ("Spark"), though the latter was only briefly innovative.

Radio and television from the time of their appearance in the Soviet Union were heavily dominated by the Communist Party apparatus and were seen as primary tools for propaganda. Until the mid-1980s most television programming consisted of either direct or indirect propaganda spiced with high art (e.g., filmed concerts and plays) and occasional grade-B thriller motion pictures.

During the glasnost period groundbreaking television programming helped create the situation in which the Soviet state was destroyed. Government control of the media began to weaken, and by 1989 official censorship had been completely abolished. A significant portion of the press was privatized, but important elements still remained under the control and regulation of the government, particularly the television news media. Among the leading newspapers, *Rossiyskaya Gazeta* ("Russian Newspaper") is the government's official organ and enjoys wide circulation. Independent newspapers, such as the weekly *Argumenty i Fakty* ("Arguments and Facts"), the daily *Moskovskii Komsomolets* ("Moscow Komsomol"), and *Nezavisimaya Gazeta* ("Independent Newspaper"), also exert influence and are widely read. *Pravda* declined in significance during the 1980s, and *Komsomolskaya Pravda* ("Komsomol Truth") and *Sovetskaya Rossiya* ("Soviet Russia") became the principal news sources for Russian communists. There are also several independent newspapers (e.g., *The Moscow Times*) that publish in English.

In the early post-Soviet years, Russian television exhibited signs of independence from the central government, but by the mid-1990s the Yeltsin government was exerting considerable influence. This trend accelerated dramatically in the Putin years. Much of Russian television is under state control; for example, Russian Public Television (Obschestvennoye Rossiyskoye Televideniye; ORT) is owned by the state, and another channel, commonly called Russian TV, is operated by the state-run Russian State Television and Radio Broadcasting Company (Vserossiyskaya Gosudartstvennaya Teleradiokompaniya). There were also several independent commercial television stations, some with wide viewership, such as Independent Television (Nezavisimoye Televideniye; NTV) and TV-6, both of which were available throughout Russia. Moreover, there were several hundred television stations that broadcast only regionally or locally. Some independently owned outlets that criticized the government found themselves the subject of official harassment during the presidency of Vladimir Putin; for example, TV-6 was ordered to cease broadcasting, and media tycoons Vladimir Gusinsky and Boris Berezovksy lost their media holdings and were forced into exile. The government operates two press agencies, ITAR-TASS, which succeeded the Soviet-era TASS agency, and the Russian Information Agency-Novosti.

# CHAPTER TWO

# THE RUSSIAN PEOPLE

A lthough ethnic Russians comprise more than four-fifths of the country's total population, Russia is a diverse, multiethnic society. More than 120 ethnic groups, many with their own national territories, speaking some 100 languages live within Russia's borders. Many of these groups are small—in some cases consisting of fewer than a thousand individuals—and, in addition to Russians, only a handful of groups have more than a million members each: the Tatars, Ukrainians, Chuvash, Bashkir, Chechens, and Armenians. The diversity of peoples is reflected in the 21 minority republics, 10 autonomous districts, and autonomous region contained within the Russian Federation. In most of these divisions, the eponymous nationality (which gives its name to the division) is outnumbered by Russians. Since the early 1990s, ethnicity has underlain numerous conflicts (e.g., in Chechnya and Dagestan) within and between these units; many national minorities have demanded more autonomy and, in a few cases, even complete independence. Those parts of Russia that do not form autonomous ethnic units are divided into various territories (*kraya*) and regions (*oblasti*), and there are two federal cities (St. Petersburg and Moscow).

**nic composition (2010)**

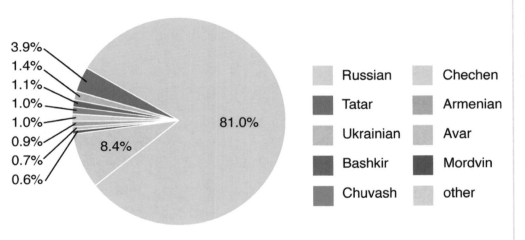

3.9%
1.4%
1.1%
1.0%
1.0%
0.9%
0.7%
0.6%

8.4%

81.0%

Russian    Chechen
Tatar      Armenian
Ukrainian  Avar
Bashkir    Mordvin
Chuvash    other

cyclopædia Britannica, Inc.

*While the majority of Russian citizens identify as ethnically Russian, there are several significant minority groups as well.*

# LANGUAGES

Linguistically, the population of Russia can be divided into the Indo-European group, comprising East Slavic speakers and smaller numbers speaking several other languages; the Altaic group, including Turkic, Manchu-Tungus, and Mongolian; the Uralic group, including Finno-Ugric and Samoyedic; and the Caucasian group, comprising Abkhazo-Adyghian and Nakho-Dagestanian. Because few of the languages of the smaller indigenous minorities are taught in the schools, it is likely that some will disappear.

## THE INDO-EUROPEAN GROUP

East Slavs—mainly Russians but including some Ukrainians and Belarusians—constitute more than four-fifths of the total population and are prevalent throughout the country. The Slavs emerged as a recognizable group in eastern Europe between the 3rd and 8th centuries CE, and the first Slav state, Kievan Rus, arose in the 9th century. After the Mongol invasions the centre of gravity shifted to Moscow, and the Russian Empire expanded to the Baltic, Arctic, and Pacific, numerically overwhelming the indigenous peoples. Despite its wide dispersal, the Russian language is homogeneous throughout Russia. Indo-Iranian speakers include the Ossetes of the Caucasus. In addition, there are sizable contingents of German speakers, who mainly populate southwestern Siberia, and Jews (recognized as an ethnolinguistic group rather than a religious one), who live mainly in European Russia; the numbers of both groups have declined through emigration.

## THE ALTAIC GROUP

Turkic speakers dominate the Altaic group. They live mainly in the Central Asian republics, but there is an important cluster of Turkic speakers between the middle Volga and southern Urals, comprising the Bashkir, Chuvash, and Tatars. A second cluster, in the North Caucasus region, includes the Balkar, Karachay, Kumyk, and Nogay. There also are numerous Turkic-speaking groups in southern Siberia between the Urals and Lake Baikal: the Altai, Khakass, Shor, Tofalar, and Tyvans (Tuvans; they inhabit the area once known as Tannu Tuva, which was annexed by the Soviet Union in 1944). The Sakha (Yakut) live mainly in the middle Lena basin, and the Dolgan are concentrated in the Arctic.

Manchu-Tungus languages are spoken by the Evenk, Even, and other small groups that are widely dispersed throughout eastern Siberia. The Buryat, who live in the Lake Baikal region, and the Kalmyk, who live primarily to the west of the lower Volga, speak Mongolian tongues.

## THE URALIC GROUP

The Uralic group, which is widely disseminated in the Eurasian forest and tundra zones, has complex origins. Finnic peoples inhabit the European section: the Mordvin, Mari (formerly Cheremis), Udmurt (Votyak) and Komi (Zyryan), and the closely related Komi-Permyaks

# THE RUSSIAN LANGUAGE

Together with Ukrainian and Belarusian, the Russian language makes up the eastern branch of the Slavic family of languages. Russian is the primary language of the overwhelming majority of people in Russia and is also used as a second language in other former republics of the Soviet Union. Russian was also taught extensively in those countries lying within the Soviet sphere of influence, especially in eastern Europe, in the second half of the 20th century.

Russian dialects are divided into the Northern group (stretching from St. Petersburg eastward across Siberia), the Southern group (in most of central and southern Russia), and the Central group (between Northern and Southern). Modern literary Russian is based on the Central dialect of Moscow, having basically the consonant system of the Northern dialect and the vowel system of the Southern dialect. The differences between these three dialects are fewer than between the dialects of most other European languages, however.

Russian and the other East Slavic languages (Ukrainian, Belarusian) did not diverge noticeably from one another until the Middle Russian period (the late 13th to the 16th century). The term "Old Russian" is generally applied to the common East Slavic language in use before that time.

Russian has been strongly influenced by Old Church Slavonic and—since the 18th-century westernizing policies of Tsar Peter I the Great—by the languages of western Europe, from which it has borrowed many words. The 19th-century poet Aleksandr Pushkin had a very great influence on the subsequent development of the language. His writings, by combining the colloquial and Church Slavonic styles, put an end to the considerable controversy that had developed as to which style of the language was best for literary uses.

The modern language uses six case forms (nominative, genitive, dative, accusative, instrumental, and locative) in the singular and plural of nouns and adjectives and expresses both a perfective aspect (completed action) and an imperfective aspect (process or incomplete action) in verbs. In its sound system the Russian language has numerous sibilant consonants and consonant clusters as well as a series of palatalized consonants contrasting with a series of unpalatalized (plain) consonants. (Palatalized consonants are those produced with simultaneous movement of the blade of the tongue toward or to the hard palate; they sound as if they have an accompanying y glide and are frequently known as soft consonants.) The reduced vowels ĭ and ŭ of the ancestral Slavic language were lost in Russian in weak position during the early historical period. Russian clause structure is basically subject–verb–object (SVO), but word order varies depending on which elements are already familiar in the discourse.

live around the upper Volga and in the Urals, while Karelians, Finns, and Veps inhabit the northwest. The Mansi (Vogul) and Khanty (Ostyak) are spread thinly over the lower Ob basin.

The Samoyedic group also has few members dispersed over a vast area: the Nenets in the tundra and forest tundra from the Kola Peninsula to the Yenisey, the Selkup around the middle Ob, and the Nganasan mainly in the Taymyr Peninsula.

## THE CAUCASIAN GROUP

There are numerous small groups of Caucasian speakers in the North Caucasus region of Russia. Abaza, Adyghian, and Kabardian (Circassian) are similar languages but differ sharply from the languages of the Nakh group (Chechen and Ingush) and of the Dagestanian group (Avar, Lezgian, Dargin, Lak, Tabasaran, and a dozen more).

## OTHER GROUPS

Several Paleo-Siberian groups that share a common mode of life but differ linguistically are located in far eastern Siberia. The Chukchi, Koryak, and Itelmen (Kamchadal) belong to a group known as Luorawetlan, which is distinct from the Eskimo-Aleut group. The languages of the Nivkh (Gilyak) along the lower Amur and on Sakhalin Island, of the Yukaghir of the Kolyma Lowland, and of the Ket of the middle Yenisey are completely isolated, though it is likely that Yukaghir is a relative of the Uralic languages.

# RELIGION

Although ethnic differences in Russia have long contained a religious element, the position of religious organizations and of their individual adherents has varied with political circumstances. In the 10th century Prince Vladimir I, who was converted by missionaries from Byzantium, adopted Christianity as the official religion for Russia, and for nearly 1,000 years thereafter the Russian

Orthodox church was the country's dominant religious institution. After the communists took power in 1917, religious institutions suffered. The church was forced to forfeit most of its property, and many monks were evicted from their monasteries. The constitution of the former Soviet Union nominally guaranteed religious freedom, but religious activities were greatly constrained, and membership in religious organizations was considered incompatible with membership in the Communist Party. Thus, open profession of religious belief was a hindrance to individual advancement. More-open expression of Christian beliefs was permitted during World War II, when the government sought the support of Christians and Jews in the fight against fascism, but restrictions were reimposed when the war ended. In the 1980s, under the reformist regime of Mikhail Gorbachev, the *glasnost* policy was declared, allowing greater toleration for the open practice of religion. The subsequent dissolution of the Soviet Union made religious freedom a reality and revealed that large sections of the population had continued to practice a variety of faiths. Indeed, Russian nationalists who emerged beginning in the 1990s identified the Russian Orthodox church as a major element of Russian culture.

Today Russian Orthodoxy is the country's largest religious denomination, representing more than half of all adherents. Organized religion was repressed by Soviet authorities for most of the 20th century, and the nonreligious still constitute more than one-fourth of the

These church officials are being greeted outside the Trinity–St. Sergius Monastery, the centre of Russian Orthodoxy, in Sergiyev Posad, Russia, north of Moscow.

population. Other Christian denominations are much smaller and include the Old Believers, who separated from the Russian Orthodox church in the 17th century, and Baptist and Evangelical groups, which grew somewhat in membership during the 20th century. Catholics, both Western rite (Roman) and Eastern rite (Uniate), and Lutherans were numerous in the former Soviet Union but lived mainly outside present-day Russia, where there are few adherents. Muslims constitute Russia's second largest religious group. In 1997 legislation was enacted that con-

# THE RUSSIAN ORTHODOX CHURCH

The largest autocephalous, or ecclesiastically independent, of the Eastern Orthodox churches is the Russian Orthodox church. Its membership is estimated at more than 85 million.

Christianity was apparently introduced into the East Slavic state of Kievan Rus by Greek missionaries from Byzantium in the 9th century. An organized Christian community is known to have existed at Kiev as early as the first half of the 10th century, and in 957 Olga, the regent of Kiev, was baptized in Constantinople. This act was followed by the acceptance of Christianity as the state religion after the baptism of Olga's grandson Vladimir, prince of Kiev, in 988. Under Vladimir's successors, and until 1448, the Russian church was headed by the metropolitans of Kiev (who after 1328 resided in Moscow) and formed a metropolitanate of the Byzantine patriarchate.

While Russia lay under Mongol rule from the 13th through the 15th century, the Russian church enjoyed a

*(Continued on the next page)*

(Continued from the previous page)

favoured position, obtaining immunity from taxation in 1270. This period saw a remarkable growth of monasticism. Finally, in 1448 the Russian bishops elected their own patriarch without recourse to Constantinople, and the Russian church was thenceforth autocephalous. In 1589 Job, the metropolitan of Moscow, was elevated to the position of patriarch with the approval of Constantinople and received the fifth rank in honour after the patriarchs of Constantinople, Alexandria, Antioch, and Jerusalem.

In the mid-17th century the Russian Orthodox patriarch Nikon attempted to establish the primacy of the Orthodox church over the state in Russia, and he also undertook a thorough revision of Russian Orthodox texts and rituals to bring them into accord with the rest of Eastern Orthodoxy. Nikon was deposed in 1666, but the Russian church retained his reforms and anathematized those who continued to oppose them; the latter became known as Old Believers and formed a vigorous body of dissenters within the Russian Orthodox church for the next two centuries.

In 1721 Tsar Peter I (the Great) abolished the patriarchate of Moscow and replaced it with the Holy Governing Synod, which was modeled after the state-controlled synods of the Lutheran church in Sweden and Prussia and was tightly controlled by the state. This control was facilitated by the political subservience of most of the higher clergy.

In November 1917, following the collapse of the tsarist government, a council of the Russian Orthodox church reestablished the patriarchate and elected the metropolitan Tikhon as patriarch. But the new Soviet government soon declared the separation of church and state and nationalized all church-held lands. These administrative measures were followed by brutal state-sanctioned persecutions that included the wholesale destruction of churches and the arrest and execution of many clerics. After Tikhon's death (1925) the government forbade patriarchal elections to be held. In 1927, in order to secure the survival of the church, Metropolitan Sergius formally expressed his "loyalty" to the Soviet government and henceforth refrained from criticizing the state in any way. This attitude of loyalty, however, provoked more divisions in the church itself: inside Russia, a number of faithful opposed Sergius, and abroad, the Russian metropolitans of America and western Europe severed their relations with Moscow. Then, in 1943, benefiting from the sudden reversal of Joseph Stalin's policies toward religion, Russian Orthodoxy underwent a resurrection; a new patriarch was elected, theological schools were opened, and thousands of churches began to function. Between 1945 and 1959 the official organization of the church was greatly expanded, although individual members of the clergy were occasionally arrested and exiled. The number of open churches reached 25,000. A new and widespread persecution of the church was subsequently instituted under the leadership of Nikita Khrushchev and Leonid Brezhnev. Then, beginning in the late 1980s, under Mikhail Gorbachev, the new political and social freedoms resulted in many church buildings being returned to the church, to be restored by local parishioners. The collapse of the Soviet Union in 1991 furthered the spiritual progress, and in 2000 Tsar Nicholas II, the Russian emperor who had been murdered by the Bolsheviks after the October Revolution of 1917, and members of his family were canonized by the church.

strained denominations outside five "traditional" religions—Russian Orthodoxy, several other Christian denominations, Islam, Judaism, and Buddhism—restricting the activities of groups not registered in the country for at least 15 years. For example, groups not meeting this requirement at the time the law was implemented (such as Roman Catholics and Mormons) were unable to operate educational institutions or disseminate religious literature.

Although there is some degree of correlation between language and religion, the two do not correspond entirely. Slavs are overwhelmingly Orthodox Christian. Turkic speakers are predominantly Muslim, although several Turkic groups in Russia are not. For example, Christianity predominates among the Chuvash, Buddhism prevails among large numbers of Altai, Khakass, and Tyvans, and many Turkic speakers east of the Yenisey have retained their shamanistic beliefs (though some have converted to Christianity). Buddhism is common among the Mongolian-speaking Buryat and Kalmyk.

Jews long suffered discrimination in Russia, including purges in the 19th century, particularly in the form of mob attacks known as pogroms. The first extensive pogroms followed the assassination of Tsar Alexander

*Ivolginsky Datsan, seen here, is the largest Buddhist temple in Russia. Located in Buryatia, it was built in the 1940s.*

II in 1881. Although the assassin was not a Jew, and only one Jew was associated with him, false rumours aroused Russian mobs in more than 200 cities and towns to attack Jews and destroy their property. In the two decades following, pogroms gradually became less prevalent; but from 1903 to 1906 they were common throughout the country.

Thereafter, to the end of the Russian monarchy, mob action against the Jews was intermittent and less widespread.

The pogrom in Kishinev (now Chisinau) in Russian-ruled Moldavia in April 1903, although more severe than most, was typical in many respects. For two days mobs, inspired by local leaders acting with official support, killed, looted, and destroyed without hindrance from police or soldiers. When troops were finally called out and the mob dispersed, 45 Jews had been killed, nearly 600 had been wounded, and 1,500 Jewish homes had been pillaged. Those responsible for inciting the outrages were not punished.

The Russian central government did not organize pogroms, as was widely believed; but the anti-Semitic policy that it carried out from 1881 to 1917 made them possible. Official persecution and harassment of Jews led the numerous anti-Semites to believe that their violence was legitimate, and their belief was strengthened by the active participation of a few high and many minor officials in fomenting attacks and by the reluctance of the government either to stop pogroms or to punish those responsible for them.

The Russian Revolution did not bring an end to the mistreatment of Russia's Jews. They suffered repression under the regime of Joseph Stalin and Nazi atrocities on Russian soil during World War II. Beginning with Gorbachev's reformist policies in the 1980s, Jewish emigration to Israel and elsewhere was permitted on an increasing scale, and the number of Jews living in Russia (and all parts of the former Soviet Union) has decreased. Prior to the breakup of the Soviet Union, about one-third of its Jewish population lived in Russia (though many did not practice Judaism), and now about one-tenth of all Jews in Russia reside in Moscow. In the 1930s Stalin established the Jewish Autonomous Region in the Soviet Far East as a Jewish province, though by the early 21st century only about 5 percent of the province's population was Jewish.

# CHAPTER THREE

# THE PERFORMING ARTS

Russia has made major contributions to all fields of the performing arts, including music, dance, theatre, and film, with the late 19th and early 20th centuries standing out as a particularly productive and influential era.

## MUSIC

Before the 18th century, Russian music was dominated by folk and church music. Secular music on a Western model began to be cultivated in the 1730s, when the Empress Anna Ivanovna imported an Italian opera troupe to entertain her court. By the end of the 18th century, there was a small body of comic operas based on Russian librettos, some by native composers and others by foreign *maestri di cappella* (Italian: "choirmasters"). The first Russian composer to gain international renown was Mikhail Glinka, a leisured aristocrat who mastered his craft in Milan and Berlin. His patriotic *A Life for the*

*Tsar* (1836) and his Pushkin-inspired *Ruslan and Lyudmila* (1842) are the oldest Russian operas that remain in the standard repertoire.

By the second half of the 19th century, an active musical life was in place, thanks mainly to the efforts of the composer and piano virtuoso Anton Rubinstein, who with royal patronage founded in St. Petersburg Russia's first regular professional orchestra (1859) and conservatory of music (1862). Both became models that were quickly imitated in other urban centres. The first major full-time professional composer in Russia was Pyotr Ilyich Tchaikovsky, a member of the initial graduating class of Rubinstein's conservatory. Tchaikovsky's powerful compositions (e.g., *Swan Lake*, *The Nutcracker*, and *The Sleeping Beauty*) are still performed widely today. Other composers of Tchaikovsky's generation were self-taught and usually earned their living in nonmusical occupations. They include Modest Mussorgsky, who worked in the civil service, Aleksandr Borodin, equally famous in his day as a chemist, and Nikolay Rimsky-Korsakov, who eventually gave up a naval career to become a professor at the St. Petersburg conservatory. The self-taught composers tended to effect a more self-consciously nationalistic style than the conservatory-bred Tchaikovsky, and among their most important works were operas such as Mussorgsky's *Boris Godunov* (final version first performed 1874) and Borodin's *Prince Igor* (first performed 1890), along with Rimsky-Korsakov's symphony *Scheherazade* (first performed 1888).

*Tchaikovsky's* Swan Lake *continues to be among the best-loved ballets. This performance of it by the Russian Royal Ballet took place in Chengdu, China, in 2010.*

Three major Russian composers emerged in the early 20th century: Aleksandr Scriabin, Sergey Rachmaninoff, and Igor Stravinsky. Scriabin, a piano virtuoso, infused his music with mysticism and evolved a modernistic idiom through which he created a musical counterpart to the Symbolist literature of the period. Rachmaninoff, also a major pianist, is best known for his concerti and for his *Rhapsody on a Theme of Paganini* (1954) for piano

and orchestra. Stravinsky, a pupil of Rimsky-Korsakov, was catapulted to early fame through his association with Serge Diaghilev, for whose Ballets Russes he composed a trio of sensational works that received their premieres in Paris: *The Firebird* (1910), *Petrushka* (1911), and *The Rite of Spring* (1913). Both Stravinsky (in 1914) and Rachmaninoff (in 1917) emigrated from Russia, first to western Europe and then to the United States, though Stravinsky made several returns to Russia toward the end of his career.

Soviet music was dominated by Sergey Prokofiev, who returned in the mid-1930s from his postrevolutionary emigration, and Dmitry Shostakovich, who spent his entire career in Soviet Russia. While living abroad Prokofiev was a modernist like Stravinsky, but he eventually adopted a more conservative, accessible idiom in

THE CULTURE OF RUSSIA

*Mischievous leaps in melody, unexpected shifts of key, and the mocking sound of reed instruments are typical of the music of Sergey Prokofiev.*

conformity with Soviet expectations. Prokofiev's most ambitious early work was the opera *The Fiery Angel* (radio premiere 1954), after a Symbolist novel by Valery Bryusov. The crowning works of his Soviet period were the ballet *Romeo and Juliet* (1935–36), the cantata *Aleksandr Nevsky* (1939; adapted from the music that he had written for Sergey Eisenstein's film of the same name), and the operatic interpretation (1942) of Tolstoy's classic novel *War and Peace*. Shostakovich is best known as a prolific composer of instrumental music, with 15 symphonies and 15 string quartets to his credit. His promising career as a stage composer was cut short when, in 1936, his very successful opera *The Lady Macbeth of the Mtsensk District*, after a novella by Nikolay Leskov, was denounced in *Pravda* ("Truth"), the official publication of the Communist Party, and banned (not to be performed again until the 1960s). He and many other Russian artists also suffered repression in the Zhdanovshchina period (1946–53), during which Soviet authorities attempted to exert greater control over art.

The best-known composers of the late- and post-Soviet period include Edison Denisov, Sofia Gubaidulina, and Alfred Schnittke. In the early 1990s Gubaidulina and Schnittke moved to Germany, where they joined other Russian émigrés. Soviet conservatories have turned out generations of world-renowned soloists. Among the best known are violinists David Oistrakh and Gidon Kremer, cellist Mstislav Rostropovich, pianists Sviatoslav Richter and Emil Gilels, and vocalist Galina Vishnevskaya. From the mid-1980s, when Mikhail Gorbachev's reform policies eased restrictions on Soviet artists, many of Russia's émigrés, such as Rostropovich and pianist Vladimir Horowitz, made triumphant returns.

Popular music also produced a number of renowned figures, not all of whom enjoyed official sanction. Particularly notable is the legacy of two "balladeers"—songwriters who performed their own works to guitar accompaniment. The raspy-voiced actor and musician Vladimir Vysotsky, whose songs circulated on thousands of bootleg cassettes throughout the 1960s and '70s, was perhaps the best-known performer in the Soviet Union until his death in 1980. Georgian Bulat Okudzhava had an almost equally loyal following. Jazz flourished with the sanction of Soviet authorities and evolved into one of the country's most popular musical forms. The Ganelin Trio, perhaps Russia's most famous jazz ensemble, toured

Western countries throughout the 1980s. The pop singer Alla Pugacheva also drew large audiences in the 1970s. Until the 1970s, rock musicians in Russia were content to reproduce not only the styles but the songs of British and American models; however, by the early 1980s Russian rock had found its native voice in the band Akvarium

## PUSSY RIOT

In February 2012 the feminist punk rock band Pussy Riot sang a controversial "punk prayer" against Putin ("Mother of God, take Putin away!") on the steps of the altar of the Cathedral of Christ the Saviour in central Moscow. Their action prompted accusations of blasphemy from the Orthodox Church and drew criminal charges. The three were found guilty of hooliganism motivated by religious hatred and sentenced to two years in prison; the trial sparked an outcry from Western governments, as well as rock stars such as Madonna, who deplored the sentences as disproportionately harsh. Their plight and their vocal anti-Putin stance resulted in their becoming probably the best-known Russian band in the West.

In October 2012 an appeals court freed one of the three women on a suspended sentence but upheld the imprisonment of the other two. In September 2013, still-imprisoned band member Nadezhda Tolokonnikova began a hunger strike after penning an open letter in which she described the exploitative treatment of inmates in the Mordovian labour camp where she was being held. In December 2013 the two remaining members and other activists were freed as part of a broad amnesty in advance of the Olympic Winter Games in Sochi, Russia.

("Aquarium"), led by charismatic songwriter and vocalist Boris Grebenshikov. The band's "concerts," played in living rooms and dormitories, were often broken up by the police, and, like Vysotsky, the band circulated its illegal music on bootleg cassettes, becoming the legendary catalyst of an underground counterculture and an inspiration to other notable bands, such as Kino. Both rock and pop music continued to flourish in post-Soviet Russia.

# DANCE AND THEATRE

Ballet was first introduced in Russia in the early 18th century, and the country's first school was formed in 1734. However, much of Russian dance was dominated by western European (particularly French and Italian) influences until the early 19th century, when Russians infused the ballet with their own folk traditions. The dramatic and ballet theatres were entirely under government control until the end of the 19th century. Actors and dancers were government employees and often were treated badly. Nevertheless, theatrical life was quite active throughout the century. Famous Russian actors and dancers of the early part of the century included the ballerina Istomina and the actor Mikhail Shchepkin. From an international perspective, however, the greatest success of the Russian theatre was in the area of classical ballet. Since the 1820s Russian dancers have reigned supreme on the ballet stage. Many great choreographers, even those of non-Russian origin, worked for the Russian Imperial Theatres, including Marius Petipa, who choreographed Tchaikovsky's

*Konstantin Stanislavsky in costume as the army officer Vershinin from the original production of Chekhov's* Three Sisters *in 1901.*

ballets *Swan Lake* and *The Sleeping Beauty.*

Producer Serge Diaghilev and directors Konstantin Stanislavsky and Vsevolod Meyerhold dominated Russian theatrical life in the first decades of the 20th century. Together with Vladimir Nemirovich-Danchenko, Stanislavsky founded the Moscow Art Theatre (later called the Moscow Academic Art Theatre) in 1898. Stanislavsky's insistence on historical accuracy, exact realism, and intense psychological preparation by his actors led to a string of successful productions from the beginning of the century into the 1930s. The theatre was known particularly for its productions of Chekhov's plays, including *The Seagull* (1896), the hit of the theatre's inaugural season.

Meyerhold was one of Stanislavsky's actors, but he broke with his master's insistence on realism. He welcomed the Russian Revolution and put his considerable talent and energy into creating a new theatre for the new state. Throughout the 1920s and into the '30s, he staged brilliant, inventive productions, both of contemporary drama and of the classics. However, his iconoclastic style fell out of favour in the 1930s, and he was arrested and executed in 1940.

Diaghilev was a brilliant organizer and impresario whose innovative Ballets Russes premiered many of the most significant ballets of the first quarter of the century. Although the legendary company was based primarily in Paris, Diaghilev employed major Russian composers (particularly Stravinsky), artists (e.g., Alexandre Benois, Natalya Goncharova, and Mikhail Larionov), and dancers (including Vaslav Nijinsky and Tamara Karsavina).

Ballet enjoyed great success in the Soviet period, not because of any innovations but because the great troupes of the Bolshoi Theatre in Moscow and the Kirov (now Mariinsky) Theatre in Leningrad (now St. Petersburg) were able to preserve the traditions of classical dance that had been perfected prior to 1917. The Soviet Union's choreography schools produced one internationally famous star after another, including the incomparable Maya Plisetskaya, Rudolf Nureyev (who defected in 1961), and Mikhail Baryshnikov (who defected in 1974).

Another extremely successful area of theatrical performance was puppet theatre. The Obraztsov Puppet Theatre (formerly the State Central Puppet Theatre), founded in Moscow by Sergey Obraztsov, continues to give delightful performances for patrons of all ages. The same can be said for the spectacular presentations of

*These puppets were among those featured in the Extraordinary Concert, a comedic show put on by the Obraztsov Puppet Theatre in 2016.*

the Moscow State Circus, which has performed throughout the world to great acclaim. Using since 1971 a larger building and renamed the Great Moscow State Circus, it excelled even in the darkest of the Cold War years.

Theatrical life in post-Soviet Russia has continued to thrive. The Moscow and St. Petersburg theatres have maintained their leading position, but they have been joined by hundreds of theatres throughout the country. Liberated from state censorship, the theatres have experimented with bold and innovative techniques and subject matter. The repertoire of the theatres experienced a shift away from political topics and toward classical and psychological themes. Since the late 1990s the Bolshoi Theatre's dominance has been challenged by the Novaya

(New) Opera Theatre in Moscow. Among other successful theatres in Moscow are the Luna Theater, Arbat-Opera, Moscow City Opera, and the Helikon-Opera.

# FILM

The Soviet cinema was a hotbed of invention in the period immediately following the 1917 revolution. Its most celebrated director was Sergey Eisenstein (a student of Meyerhold), whose great films include *Battleship Potemkin* and *Ivan the Terrible*. Eisenstein also was a student of filmmaker and theorist Lev Kuleshov, who formulated the groundbreaking editing process called montage at the world's first film school, the All-Union Institute of Cinematography in Moscow. Supported by Vladimir Lenin (the founder of the Russian Communist Party and the first leader of the Soviet Union), who recognized film's ability to communicate his revolutionary message to illiterate and non-Russian-speaking audiences, the school initially trained filmmakers in the art of agitprop (agitation and propaganda). Like Eisenstein, who incorporated the Marxist dialectic in his theory of editing, another of Kuleshov's students, Vsevolod Illarionovich Pudovkin, made his mark on motion picture history primarily through his innovative use of montage, especially in his masterwork, *Mother* (1926). Similarly important was Dziga Vertov, whose *kino-glaz* ("film-eye") theory—that the camera, like the human eye, is best used to explore real life—had a huge impact on the development of documentary filmmaking and cinema realism in the 1920s.

*A movie poster for Battleship Potemkin. The film is based on the mutiny of Russian sailors against their tyrannical superiors aboard the battleship Potemkin during the Revolution of 1905.*

Film did not escape the strictures of Socialist Realism, but a few post-World War II films in this style were artistically successful, including *The Cranes Are Flying* (1957; directed by Mikhail Kalatozov) and *Ballad of a Soldier* (1959; directed by Grigory Chukhrai). A number of successful film versions of classic texts also were made in the 1950s and '60s, particularly Grigory Kozintsev's spectacular versions of *Hamlet* (1964) and *King Lear* (1971). Prominent among the notable Russian directors who emerged in the 1960s and '70s were Andrey Tarkovsky (*Ivan's Childhood* [1962], *Andrey Rublev* [1966], *Solaris* [1971], and *Nostalgia* [1983]) and the Georgian-born Armenian Sergey Paradzhanov (*Shadows of Forgotten Ancestors* [1964] and *The Colour of Pomegranates* [1969]).

The 1980s and '90s were a period of crisis in the Russian cinema. Although Russian filmmakers were free from the diktat of the communist authorities, the industry suffered from drastically reduced state subsidies. The state-controlled film-distribution system also collapsed, and this led to the dominance of Western films in Russia's theatres. Private investment did not quickly take the place of subsidies, and many in Russia complained that the industry often produced elitist films primarily for foreign film festivals while the public was fed a steady diet of second-rate movies.

Nonetheless, Russian cinema continued to receive international recognition. Two films—Vladimir Menshov's *Moscow Does Not Believe in Tears* (1979) and Nikita Mikhalkov's *Burnt by the Sun* (1994)—received the Acad-

# SERGEY EISENSTEIN

He has been called the epic poet of the Soviet cinema, and many consider Sergey Eisenstein the finest craftsman ever to direct motion pictures. His films *Battleship Potemkin*, released in 1925, *Alexander Nevsky* (1938), and *Ivan the Terrible* (Part One, 1944; Part Two, completed 1946, released 1958) are classics of movie art. Among his other films were *October*, or *Ten Days That Shook the World* (1928), the story of the Russian Revolution; *Old and New* (1929), on Soviet agriculture; and *Sentimental Melody* (1929). He also wrote several books on directing.

Eisenstein was born in Riga, Latvia, on January 23, 1898. Twelve years later the family settled in St. Petersburg, where he attended the Institute of Civil Engineering and the School of Fine Arts. During the Russian Revolution he helped organize defense and provided entertainment for the troops. Following the war he became assistant decorator at the Theater of the People. Soon he was chief decorator and then codirector. His first film, *Strike*, was released in 1924. In this and other movies he proposed a new way of filming—what he called the "montage of attractions"—in which arbitrarily chosen images were presented not in chronological sequence but in whatever way they created the maximum psychological impact. The effect was striking, but the objective reality was falsified.

Possessed by his theory, Eisenstein was bound to succumb often to this failing. *Battleship Potemkin*, also called just *Potemkin*, happily escaped it. Ordered by the Central Executive Committee of the U.S.S.R. to commemorate the Revolution of 1905, the film, made in the port and the city of Odessa in 1925, had a momentous impact and still remains among the masterpieces of the world cinema. (In 1958 it was voted the best film ever made, by an international poll of critics.) Its greatness lies not merely in the depth of humanity with which the subject is treated, nor in its social significance, nor in the formal perfection of its rhythm and editing; but rather, it is each of these magnified and multiplied by the others.

Having expressed contrition for the errors of his past works, Eisenstein was able to make a film recounting the medieval epic of *Alexander Nevsky*, in accordance with Stalin's policy of glorifying Russian heroes. Made in 1938, this film transfigured the actual historical events, majestically leading to a final resolution that represented the triumph of collectivism. As in medieval epics, the characters were the strongly stylized heroes or demigods of legend. Produced in close collaboration with Prokofiev, who wrote the score, the film represented a blend of images and music into a single rhythmic unity, an indissoluble whole.

During World War II Eisenstein achieved a work of the same style as *Alexander Nevsky* and even more ambitious— *Ivan the Terrible*—about the 16th-century tsar Ivan IV, whom Stalin admired. Begun in 1943 in the Ural Mountains, the first part was finished in 1944, the second at the beginning of 1946. A third part was envisaged, but Eisenstein, suffering from angina pectoris, had to take to his bed for several months. He was about to return to work when he died, only a few days after his 50th birthday.

Most critics would agree that though Eisenstein's three greatest films stand far above the others, all of his work is significant; their flaws are those common to artists probing the limits of their craft. It may be that in the entire history of motion pictures, no other filmmaker has surpassed him in his understanding of his art.

emy Award for best foreign-language film. The work of Andrey Konchalovsky, who has plied his craft in Russia as well as in Europe and the United States with features such as *Runaway Train* (1985) and *House of Fools* (2002), is also highly regarded. In the late 1990s Aleksandr Sokurov emerged as a director of exceptional talents, gaining international acclaim for *Mother and Son* (1997) and *Russian Ark* (2002), the first feature film ever to be shot in a single take. His 2011 film, *Faust*, was widely acclaimed.

# CHAPTER FOUR

# THE VISUAL ARTS

For centuries, all of the visual art Russia produced was religious in nature. Under Peter the Great, secular subjects were introduced and European influence became dominant. By the early 20th century, Russian artists such as Vasily Kandinsky and Kazimir Malevich were playing a major role in the European art scene.

## MEDIEVAL RUSSIAN ART

The Novgorod school of Russian medieval icon and mural painting flourished around the northwestern city of Novgorod from the 12th through the 16th century. A thriving merchant city, Novgorod was the cultural centre of Russia during the Mongol occupation of most of the rest of the country in the 13th and 14th centuries. During that period it preserved the Byzantine traditions that formed the basis of Russian art and at the same time fostered the development of a distinct and vital local style, a style which, though provincial, contained most of the

Miracle of St. George over the Dragon, *an icon by an anony-mous artist of the Novgorod school, was painted at the begin-ning of the 15th century. It now hangs in the State Tretyakov Gallery, in Moscow.*

elements of the national Russian art that eventually developed in Moscow in the 16th century.

The first important phase of the Novgorod school lasted through the 12th century and the first half of the 13th, a period during which the Byzantine tradition spread from southern Kiev, the first capital and cultural centre of Russia, to the northern centres of Novgorod and Vladimir-Suzdal. In this period fresco painting was the dominant art form. In the second half of the 12th century the hieratic, aristocratic artistic tradition of Kiev was abandoned in favour of a more informal approach that combined Byzantine severity of style with a tenderness of gesture and an anecdotal picturesqueness. This spirit was matched in the beginning of the 13th century by a shift toward lighter, brighter colours and flatter forms, a softening of facial types, and an increasing definition of form by means of a graceful, rhythmic line. The progressive importance of line over modeled form in Novgorod painting brought about a gradual change in the Byzantine image. Strongly modeled Byzantine figures were characterized by a direct and penetrating gaze that in turn engaged that of the viewer. But as the predominance of line flattened the figures and faces in Novgorod painting, the direct gaze receded into a dreamy, abstracted, introspective look. In addition, the line invited a contemplation of its abstract patterns; Novgorod painting began to emphasize the lyricism of these patterns rather than the immediate presence of the figures.

In the early 14th century, a new artistic impetus was provided by the introduction of the iconostasis, a screen standing before the sanctuary on which icons, formerly scattered over the walls of the church, could be hung in a prescribed arrangement. The stylistic tendencies of the previous period of artistic activity, which had been dominated by fresco painting, were brought to bear on the visual problems created by the iconostasis and coalesced into a definitive Novgorod style. The complex of paintings on the iconostasis demanded a coherent overall impression. This overall effect was achieved through the use of strong, rhythmic lines and colour harmonies in each icon. Novgorod painters used jewellike juxtapositions of brilliant yet delicately balanced colours, dominated by yellow, emerald green, and fiery vermilion. The silhouette became all-important, as did the line, which assumed unprecedented grace with an elongation of the figure that became standard in Russian art. A number of Greek artists who arrived from Constantinople at the end of the 14th century brought a more varied subject matter to the Novgorod school and introduced the use of more complex architectural backgrounds. The most influential of these Byzantine immigrants was a mural painter, Theophanes the Greek. Theophanes contributed a greater understanding of the human form and a subtler use of colour and design to later Novgorod painting.

At the end of the 15th century Novgorod painting became somewhat repetitive, and, although works of outstanding quality continued to be produced, they lacked the freshness of the earlier paintings. The leadership in Russian painting passed in the 16th century to the more cosmopolitan art of the Moscow school, and the final dissolution of the Novgorod school came with the forcible transfer of Novgorod artists to Moscow after a fire in the capital in 1547.

The Moscow school succeeded the Novgorod school as the dominant Russian school of painting and eventually developed the stylistic basis for a national art. Moscow began a local artistic development parallel to that of Novgorod and other centres as it rose to a leading position in the movement to expel the Mongols, who had occupied most of Russia since the mid-13th century. The autocratic tradition of the city fostered from the beginning a preference for abstracted spiritual expression over practical narrative.

The first flowering of the Moscow school occurred under the influence of the painter Theophanes the

Greek, who was born and trained in Constantinople (Istanbul), assimilated the Russian manner and spirit at Novgorod, and moved from Novgorod to Moscow about 1400. Theophanes went far beyond contemporary models in complexity of composition, subtle beauty of colour, and the fluid, almost impressionistic rendering of his deeply expressive figures. His achievements instilled in Muscovite painting a permanent appreciation of curving planes. Theophanes' most important successor was the most

*Andrey Rublyov's* The Saviour *dates to 1411 and can now be seen in the State Tretyakov Gallery, in Moscow.*

distinguished of Russia's medieval painters, a monk, Andrey Rublyov, who painted pictures of overwhelming spirituality and grace in a style that owes almost nothing to Theophanes except a devotion to artistic excellence. He concentrated on delicacy of line and luminous colour; he eliminated all unnecessary detail to strengthen the impact of the composition, and he constructed remarkably subtle and complex relationships among the few forms that remained. Elements of Rublyov's art are reflected in most of the finest Moscow paintings of the 15th century.

The period from the time of Rublyov's death, about 1430, to the end of the 15th century was marked by a sudden growth in Moscow's prestige and sophistication. The grand dukes of Moscow finally drove out the Mongols and united most of the cities of central Russia, including Novgorod, under their leadership. With the fall of Constantinople to the Turks in 1453, Moscow, for some time the centre of the Russian Orthodox church, became the virtual centre of Eastern Orthodoxy. An artist whose career reflected the new sophistication was the major painter Dionisy, a layman. Dionisy's compositions, based more on intellect than on an instinctive expression of spirituality, are more arresting than either Theophanes' or Rublyov's. His figures convey an effect of extreme elongation and buoyancy through a drastic reduction, by simplified drawing, to silhouette and through a disparate spacing that spreads them out in a processional effect, breaking with the earlier Russian predilection for tight composition. There is a subtle colour scheme of turquoise, pale green, and rose against darker blues and purples. Perhaps the most significant quality of Dionisy's painting was his ability to emphasize the mystical over the dramatic content of narrative scenes.

The new prestige of the Russian Orthodox church led to an unprecedented seriousness in the mystical interpretation of traditional subject matter; by the mid-16th century there were specific directives from the church based on a new didactic iconography that expounded mysteries, rites, and dogmas. The general stylistic traditions already established were followed throughout the 16th and 17th centuries, but icons became smaller and crowded in composition and steadily declined in quality. By the late 16th century much of the former spirituality had been lost, replaced by decorative enrichment.

At the beginning of the 17th century the so-called Stroganov school of Moscow artists assumed the leadership of the last phase of Russian medieval art. The original patrons of this group of artists were the wealthy Stroganov family, colonizers in northeastern Russia; but the artists perfected their work in the service of the tsar and his family in Moscow. The Stroganov school produced not so much a coherent style as a type of icon. Designed specifically for private use, this type was characterized by its small size, its miniature technique, and its exquisite refinement of detail. The icons of the Stroganov school, while retaining Byzantine-inspired Russian forms, nevertheless represent a radical departure from most of what had been valued in the long tradition of Russian painting; monumentality was replaced by precious virtuosity and deep emotion by decorative elegance. The preoccupation with style and technique over content was, perhaps, typical of the end of a cultural phase.

In its richness and refinement, the art of the Stroganov school reflected the tastes of royal and noble patrons. Working in a muted colour range dominated by golden brown, the Stroganov masters substituted for the colouristic brilliance of the earlier Russian tradition a lavish use of gold and silver linear highlights whose strongly abstract patterns matched the mannered fragility of the figures. They embellished their icons with frames and halos of beaten gold and silver. The naturalism proscribed by the church for major representations was ingeniously introduced by the Stroganov school in background details of architecture, vegetation, and even atmospheric effects. The Stroganov masters excelled at composition; though their works are very small and sometimes include many figures, they never appear crowded.

The Stroganov school remained influential until the end of the 17th century, but after about 1650 it gradually declined. The foundation of the new capital of St. Petersburg in 1703 by Peter I the Great marked a turning point in Russian art: although icon painting continued to follow the Russo-Byzantine tradition throughout the 19th century, the major artistic activity shifted to secular art and Europe's Baroque style.

## THE 19TH AND 20TH CENTURIES

With the exception of the portraitist Dmitry Levitsky, no great Russian painters emerged in the 18th and early 19th centuries. In the 1830s the Russian Academy of Arts (which had been founded in 1757) began sending Russian painters abroad for training. Among the most gifted of these were Aleksandr Ivanov and Karl Bryullov, both of whom were known for Romantic historical canvases. A truly national tradition of painting did not begin, however, until the 1870s with the appearance of the "Itinerants." Although their work is not well known outside Russia, the serene landscapes of Isaak Levitan, the expressive portraits of Ivan Kramskoy and Ilya Repin, and the socially oriented genre paintings of Vladimir Makovsky, Vasily Perov, and Repin arguably deserve an international reputation.

As with literature, there was a burst of creativity in the visual arts in the early 20th century, with Russian painters playing a major role in the European art scene. This period was marked by a turning away from realism to primitivism, Symbolism, and abstract painting. Members of the Jack of Diamonds group of artists advocated the most advanced European avant-garde trends in their own painting and exhibited works by European artists such as Albert Gleizes and Ernst Ludwig Kirchner. Vasily Kandinsky created his highly influential lyrical abstractions during this period, while Kazimir Malevich began to explore the rigid, geometric abstraction of Suprematism. In his first Suprematist work, a pencil drawing of a black square on a white field, all the elements of objective representation that had characterized his earlier, Cubo-Futurist style—a distinctly Russian offshoot movement blending Cubism and Futurism—had been eliminated. Malevich explained that "the appropriate means of representation is always the one which gives fullest possible expression to feeling as such and which ignores the familiar appearance of objects." Referring to his first Suprematist work (*Black Square*, 1915), he identified

The Knife Grinder, *or* Principle of Glittering, *by Kazimir Malevich, dates from 1912–13. It now hangs in the Yale University Art Gallery, in New Haven, Connecticut.*

the black square with feeling and the white background with expressing "the void beyond this feeling."

During this same period Marc Chagall began his life-long pursuit of poetic, whimsical paintings based on his

# VASILY KANDINSKY

The Russian painter Vasily Kandinsky is generally regarded as one of the originators of abstract painting. In both his painting and his theoretical writings he influenced modern styles.

Kandinsky was born in Moscow on December 4, 1866. After a visit in 1895 to an exhibition of French impressionist paintings in Moscow, Kandinsky decided to become a painter. Moving to Munich, Germany, he worked under Anton Azbé and Franz von Stuck. He studied impressionist color and art nouveau (an ornamental style of about 1890 to 1910). From the very beginning Kandinsky's work showed an interest in fantasy. He began developing his ideas concerning the power of pure color and nonrepresentational painting. In 1909 Kandinsky helped found the New Artists' Association in Munich.

Kandinsky painted his first abstract watercolor in 1910 and began formulating his important theoretical study, *Concerning the Spiritual in Art*, which was published originally in German in 1912. In this work he examined the psychological effects of color and made comparisons between painting and music. Together with the German painter Franz Marc, Kandinsky became a leader in the influential Blaue Reiter (Blue Rider) movement, an expressionist group. He and Marc edited a Blue Rider almanac in which they reproduced art from all ages.

With the outbreak of World War I, Kandinsky left Germany to return to Russia, where he taught and organized numerous artistic activities. He returned to Germany in 1921 and became one of the principal teachers at the Bauhaus school in Weimar. A change took place in Kandinsky's work during the 1920s. From the romantic superabundance of his earlier

*(Continued on the next page)*

(Continued from the previous page)

abstract expressionism, his style evolved to feature geometric forms—points, bundles of lines, circles, and triangles.

He remained with the school until it was closed by the Nazi regime in 1933. Kandinsky then moved to a Parisian suburb, where he stayed until his death on December 13, 1944. During the last decade of his life, Kandinsky blended the free, intuitive images of his earlier years with the geometric forms of his Bauhaus period.

own personal mythology, work that defies classification within any one group or trend. Along with being a painter, Chagall was a printmaker and designer. He composed his images based on emotional and poetic associations, rather than on rules of pictorial logic. Predating Surrealism, his early works, such as *I and the Village* (1911), were among the first expressions of psychic reality in modern art. His works in various media include sets for plays and ballets, etchings illustrating the Bible, and stained-glass windows. Chagall's repertory of images, including massive bouquets, melancholy clowns, flying lovers, fantastic animals, biblical prophets, and fiddlers on roofs, helped to make him one of the most popular major innovators of the 20th-century School of Paris. He presented dreamlike subject matter in rich colours and in a fluent, painterly style that—while reflecting an awareness of artistic movements such as Expressionism, Cubism, and even abstraction—remained invariably personal.

*Marc Chagall works on his painting* Commedia dell' Arte. *Although he borrowed elements from Cubism, Impressionism, and Fauvism, Chagall's style cannot be classified with any artistic movement of his time.*

The 1920s were a period of continued experimentation. Perhaps the most noteworthy movement was Constructivism. The Constructivists favoured strict geometric forms and crisp graphic design. Many became actively involved in the task of creating living spaces and forms of daily life; they designed furniture, ceramics, and clothing, and they worked in graphic design and architecture. The movement is generally considered to have been initiated in 1913 with the "painting reliefs"—abstract geometric constructions—of Vladimir Tatlin. The expatriate Russian sculptors Antoine Pevsner and Naum Gabo joined Tatlin and his followers in Moscow, and upon publication of their jointly written *Realist Manifesto* in 1920 they became the spokesmen of the movement. It is from the manifesto that the name Constructivism was derived; one of the directives that it contained was "to construct" art. Because of their admiration for machines and technology, functionalism, and modern industrial materials such as plastic, steel, and glass, members of the movement were also called artist-engineers. Non-Constructivist artists, including Pavel Filonov and Mariya Ender, also produced major works in this period.

By the end of the 1920s, however, the same pressures that confronted experimental writing were brought to bear on the visual arts. With the imposition of Socialist Realism, the great painters of the early 1920s found themselves increasingly isolated. Eventually, their works were removed from museums, and in many cases the artists themselves were almost completely forgotten. Experimental art was replaced by countless pictures of Lenin—as, for example, Isaak Brodsky's *Lenin at the Smolny* (1930)—and by a seemingly unending string of rose-tinted Socialist Realist depictions of everyday life bearing titles like *The Tractor Drivers' Supper* (1951). It was not until the late 1980s that the greatest works of Russian art of the early 20th century were again made available to the public.

The visual arts took longer to recover from the Stalinist years than did literature. It was not until the 1960s and '70s that a new group of artists, all of whom worked "underground," appeared. Major artists included Ernst Neizvestny, Ilya Kabakov, Mikhail Shemyakin, and Erik Bulatov. They employed techniques as varied as primitivism, hyperrealism, grotesque, and abstraction, but they shared a common distaste for the canons of Socialist Realism.

*Ernst Neizvestny's* Mask of Grief, *also translated as the* Mask of Sorrow, *honors those who died in the Gulag (labor camps) of the Magadan region.*

By the late 1980s a large number of Russian artists had emigrated, and many became well known on the world art scene. Particularly notable was the team of Vitaly Komar and Alex Melamid, who became internationally recognized during the 1990s for a project in which they systematically—and ironically—documented what various people throughout the world said they valued most in a painting.

Photography has grown in importance in the 21st century. The exploration of national identity was the theme of "Anastasia Khoroshilova: Russkie" at the Moscow Museum of Modern Art in 2008–2009. Her exhibition comprised more than 100 portraits of individuals and family groups chosen to emphasize the ethnic diversity within contemporary Russia.

# CHAPTER FIVE

# RUSSIAN ARCHITECTURE

From onion-domed churches to the apartment blocks of the Soviet era, Russia has produced a wealth of architecture that is recognizably Russian.

## THE BYZANTINE INFLUENCE

Kievan Rus was converted to Christianity in 988, and in Kiev, its dominant political and cultural centre, mosaics dating from about 1045 were created by Byzantine craftsmen. From Kiev the Byzantine style of architecture soon spread throughout the principalities of Novgorod and Vladimir-Suzdal. The emphasis of the Byzantine church on the physical splendour of its edifices was a cardinal factor in determining the characteristics of Russian ecclesiastical architecture. Everything connected with the design and decoration of the new churches followed the Byzantine pattern; and the standard scheme of the Greek church—the cross inscribed in a rectangle and the dome supported on piers or on pendentives—became the accepted type for Orthodox churches. The design and support of the central dome or cupola, together with the number and disposition of the subsidiary cupolas, remained for a long time the principal theme of Russian architecture.

Novgorod was the centre of a unique and quite original art that lived on long after the political death of the city in the 16th century; it was there that the fundamental features of later Russian architecture were developed. The ecclesiastical architectural history of Novgorod began with the Cathedral of St. Sophia. It was built in 1045–52, replacing a wooden, 13-dome church of the same name. The new cathedral's divergences from the Byzantine pattern are quite apparent; it has double aisles but only three apses. The church has only cupolas, its walls are austere, the buttresses are flat and bare, and the windows are small and narrow.

The churches of the 12th century resemble St. Sophia, Novgorod, only in the general tendency toward simplicity and verticality; they were small, cubic in form, and modest in decoration. The severe climate and heavy snowfalls of the north necessitated various modifications of the Byzantine architectural forms. In the course of time windows were narrowed and deeply splayed; roofs became steeper; and flat-dome profiles assumed the bulbous form, which, in different varieties, eventually became the most notable feature of Russian church architecture.

The churches of Pskov in northwest Russia were relatively tiny and squat and usually had three low

*The Cathedral of St. Sophia in Novgorod. There is something unmistakably Russian in the silhouette of its helmeted cupolas and in the vigour and verticality of its solid masses.*

apses. The cupolas, roofs, and decorative elements were similar to those of Novgorod. Because these churches were too small to contain interior columns for the support of the cupola, the Pskov builders developed the structural device of recessive rows of corbel arches (stepped archlike structures built out from the walls) for the support of cupola drums and cupolas. This feature—the *kokoshniki*—was to become a favourite Russian structural and decorative element. The church porches, the exterior walled-in galleries, and the arcaded bell towers were Pskov's other outstanding contributions to Russian architecture.

The region of Vladimir-Suzdal (also in northwest Russia), as another centre of early Russian culture, was a factor in a creative fusion of Byzantine, Romanesque, and Caucasian influences—the Romanesque being seen in the style that was growing up in western Europe and the Caucasian influence appearing in the churches to the south. The 12th- and early 13th-century structures were a further modification of the earlier Byzantine style, leading toward the innovations at Moscow in the 15th century.

After Constantinople fell to the Turks in 1453, Russia continued for several centuries to develop a national art that had grown out of the middle Byzantine period. During the 10th–15th centuries, Russian art had begun to show marked local variation from the Byzantine model, and after the fall of Constantinople it continued along these distinctive lines of development. This period of Russian art, which lasted until the adoption of western European culture in the 18th century, is also known as the Moscow or National period.

After the hegemony in the world of Orthodox Christianity shifted to Muscovite Russia, Moscow, having become the new city of Constantine—the "third Rome"—and aspiring to rival the older centres of culture, launched a building program commensurate with its international importance. The Kremlin and two of its important churches were rebuilt by Italian architects between 1475 and 1510. These churches, the Assumption

(Uspensky) Cathedral and the cathedral of St. Michael the Archangel, were largely modeled after the churches of Vladimir. The Italians were required to incorporate the basic features of Byzantine planning and design into the new cathedrals; it was only in the exterior decoration of St. Michael the Archangel that they succeeded in introducing Italian decorative motifs. A third church, the modest Annunciation Cathedral (1484–89), with its warm beauty, was the work of Pskov architects. There the *kokoshniki* were introduced in the treatment of the roof. This element, similar in outline to the popular Russian *bochka* roof (pointed on top, with the sides forming a continuous double curve, concave above and convex below), foreshadowed a tendency to replace the forms of the Byzantine arch by more elongated silhouettes. Ecclesiastical architecture began to lose the special features associated with the Byzantine heritage, becoming more national in character and increasingly permeated with the taste and thought of the people. The most important change in Russian church design of the 16th century was the introduction of the tiered tower and the tent-shaped roof first developed in wood by Russia's carpenters. Next was the substitution of the bulb-shaped spire for the traditional Byzantine cupola. This affected the design of masonry architecture by transforming its proportions and decoration and even its structural methods. The buildings acquired a dynamic, exteriorized articulation and specifically Russian national characteristics.

The boldest departures from Byzantine architecture were the Church of the Ascension at Kolomenskoye (now a suburb of Moscow; 1532), the Church of the Decapitation of St. John the Baptist at Dyakovo (*c.* 1532), and, above all, the cathedral of St. Basil (Vasily) the Blessed in Moscow (1554–60).

In St. Basil the western academic architectural concepts, based on rational, manifest harmony, were ignored; the structure, with no easily readable design and a profusion of disparate colourful exterior decoration, is uniquely medieval Russian in content and form and in technique, decoration, and feeling. St. Basil, like its predecessors, the churches at Kolomenskoye and Dyakovo, embodies the characteristic features of the wood churches of northern Russia, translated into masonry. An effective finishing touch was given to the ensemble of the Kremlin's Cathedral Square by the erection of the imposing Assumption Belfry, begun in 1532 and built as a complement to the adjacent Ivan the Great Bell Tower. The colossal white stone "column of fame," with its golden cupola gleaming above the Kremlin hill, was the definite expression of an era, reflecting the tastes and grandiose political ambitions of the rising Russian state.

The basic types and structural forms of the Russian multicolumned and tented churches were fully developed in the 16th century. It remained for the next century to concentrate its efforts on the refinement of those forms and on the embellishment of the facades. The tent spires degenerated into mere decoration; they were used as exterior ornamental features set loosely in numbers over gabled roofs and on top of roof vaulting (for example, the church of the Nativity in Putinki in Moscow, 1649–52). This decorative use of the formerly functional element was combined with the liberal employment of the *kokoshnik*. The latter, in converging and ascending tiers and in diversified shapes and arrangements, was used as a decorative screen for the drumlike bases of the spires and sometimes as parapets over the cornices. At the same time the formerly large expanses of unbroken wall surfaces (of the Novgorod-Pskov architectural traditions) were replaced by rich decorative paneling. Polychromy asserted itself: coloured and glazed tile and carved stone ornament, used in combination with brick patterns, were employed extensively. This was especially evidenced in a large group of Yaroslavl churches.

## THE BAROQUE

The Baroque appeared in Russia toward the end of the 17th century. The Russians imaginatively transformed its modes into a clearly expressed national style that became known as the Naryshkin Baroque, a delightful example of which is the church of the Intercession of the Virgin at Fili (1693) on the estate of Boyarin Naryshkin, whose name had become identified with this phase of the Russian Baroque.

Western Europeans brought the prevailing Baroque styles characteristic of their own countries, but the very different artistic and physical setting of St. Petersburg produced a new expression, embodying Russia's peculiar sense of form, scale, colour, and choice of materials. The transformed Baroque eventually spread all over Russia and, with its vast register of variations, developed many regional idioms.

A French architect, Nicolas Pineau, went to Russia in 1716 and introduced the Rococo style to the newly founded city of St. Petersburg (e.g., Peter's study in Peterhof, before 1721). The Rococo in Russia flourished in St. Petersburg under the protection of Peter I and Elizabeth. Peter's principal architect, Gaetano Chiaveri, who drew heavily on northern Italian models, is most noted for the library of the Academy of Sciences (1725) and the royal

*The Baroque Grand Palace (1714–28) was designed by Domenico Trezzini and the palace's gardens by Alexandre Le Blond. Bartolomeo Rastrelli enlarged the structure in 1752.*

churches of Warsaw and Dresden. Bartolomeo Rastrelli was responsible for all large building projects under the reign of Elizabeth, and among his most accomplished designs in St. Petersburg are the Smolny Cathedral and the turquoise and white Winter Palace.

# NEOCLASSICAL ARCHITECTURE

The leading role played by Russia in the production of early Neoclassical architecture was almost entirely due to Catherine II (also known as Catherine the Great). Under her aegis St. Petersburg was transformed into an unparalleled museum of Neoclassical buildings as advanced as contemporary French and English work. As in other countries, the new taste for antique simplicity represented a reaction against the excesses of the Rococo, which in Russia had its apotheosis in the work of Bartolomeo Francesco Rastrelli.

Two foreign architects played important roles: a Scotsman, Charles Cameron, whose most extensive work was at Tsarskoye Selo in the style invented by Robert Adam and who was responsible for introducing the first correct Greek Doric column and entablature in Russia in the circular Temple of Friendship at Pavlovsk (1780); and an Italian, Giacomo Antonio Domenico Quarenghi, who arrived in Russia in 1780 and built for Catherine the Palladian English Palace at Peterhof (1781–89).

The two leading Russian architects were Vasily Ivanovich Bazhenov and Ivan Yegorovich Starov, both of whom studied in Paris under de Wailly in the 1760s,

# GIACOMO ANTONIO DOMENICO QUARENGHI

An Italian-born Neoclassical architect and painter, Giacomo Antonio Domenico Quarenghi is best known as the builder of numerous works in Russia during and immediately after the reign of Catherine the Great. He was named "Grand Architect of all the Russias."

The son of a painter, Quarenghi was born on September 20, 1744, at Rota d'Imagna in the Republic of Venice (in what is now Italy). He studied painting first in Bergamo and then in Rome, where he was taught by Anton Raphael Mengs and Stefano Pozzi. Vincenzo Brenna introduced Quarenghi to architecture. In 1779 Baron Friedrich Grimm secured Quarenghi's invitation to Russia by the empress Catherine II.

Among his first important commissions were the English Palace at Peterhof (1781–89), since destroyed, and the Hermitage Theatre (begun 1782). These were the first buildings in Russia in the Palladian style. Other early constructions include the massive Bourse and the State Bank (1789–96).

His other works in St. Petersburg included St. George's Hall in the Winter Palace (1786–95), several bridges on the Neva, and a number of academic structures, including the Academy of Sciences (1785–90), the Catherine Institute (1804–07; now the Saltykov-Shchedrin Library), and the Smolny Institute (1806–08). At the royal residence of Tsarskoye Selo (now Pushkin), Quarenghi designed the baths, concert hall, church, the Alexander Palace, and other structures.

Quarenghi designed simple but imposing Neoclassical buildings that have clear and precise designs. His favourite format was a plain rectangular block fronted by an elegant central portico with pillars and pediment. His buildings give the city of St. Petersburg much of its stately character.

bringing back to Russia the most-advanced Neoclassical ideas. Bazhenov designed the new Arsenal in St. Petersburg (1765) and prepared unexecuted designs for the Kamenni Ostrov Palace (1765–75) and for a new Kremlin. Starov designed a country house for Prince Gagarin at Nikolskoye (1774–76), the new cathedral of the Trinity, St. Petersburg (1776), and the influential prototype of Russian country houses, the Tauride Palace (1783–88), for Grigory Potemkin, Catherine's lover. The Tauride Palace consisted of a central-domed and porticoed central block connected by narrow galleries to large wings.

Under Catherine's grandson, Alexander I (reigned 1801–25), the Russian version of the Empire style flourished. The great monument of this later period was the St. Petersburg Bourse (1804–16) by Thomas de Thomon, a vast peripteral (surrounded by a row of columns) edifice. Andrey Nikiforovich Voronikhin, also a pupil of de Wailly, was architect of the Kazan Cathedral, St. Petersburg (1801–11), and Andreyan Dmitriyevich Zakharov built the Admiralty (1806–15) in the same city.

# THE COMMUNIST PERIOD

The architecture of Russia in the 19th century developed as the Slavic Revival focused on the medieval art and the affirmation of Russian heritage. New interpretative approaches came, in particular, with the mass construction of railway stations, such as Moscow Rail Terminal on the Nevsky Prospect (1851) in St. Petersburg, and by several of the older railway terminals in Moscow dating from the second half of the 19th century, including Leningrad Station (originally Nikolaevskiy; 1844–51). The Cathedral of Christ the Saviour (Moscow), consecrated in 1883, was an imposing monument; it was destroyed by the Soviets in 1932 and rebuilt in the 1990s.

In the period after the Russian Revolution of 1917 the erstwhile Soviet Union at first encouraged modern art, and several architects, notably the German Bruno Taut, looked to the new government for a sociological program. The Constructivist project for a *Monument to the Third International* (1920) by Vladimir Tatlin was a machine in which the various sections (comprising legislative houses and

*This reconstruction of the* Monument to the Third International *model, designed by Vladimir Tatlin in 1920, was built in Sweden in 1968.*

offices) would rotate within an exposed steel armature. A workers' club in Moscow (1929) had a plan resembling half a gear, and the Ministry of Central Economic Planning (1928–32), designed by Le Corbusier, was intended to be a glass-filled slab but, because of Stalin's dislike of modern architecture, was never completed. Its foundation later was used for an outdoor swimming pool.

Modern European styles of architecture were subjected to official disfavour in the Soviet Union in the 1930s, as Stalin's government adopted Classical monuments—such as Boris Mikhaylovich Iofan's winning design for the Palace of the Soviets (1931), which was intended to pile Classical colonnades to a height of 1,365 feet (416 metres) and have a colossal statue of Lenin at its summit. With its gigantic Corinthian columns, the building for the Central Committee of the Communist Party at Kiev (1937) showed an overbearing scale.

Bland, monumental housing projects dominated the architectural production of the postwar period; later in the century such structures were increasingly seen as eyesores, however, and a new generation of architects focused on creating buildings that fit their contexts, often combining elements of European and Russian traditions. Beginning in the mid-1980s, aided by liberalization, artistic experimentation began a resurgence within Russia, and many Russian painters enjoyed successful exhibitions both at home and abroad.

# CHAPTER SIX

# RUSSIAN LITERATURE

Russian literature has a long and rich tradition. The term "Russian literature" is used to describe the literature of different areas at different periods, from the loose confederation of East Slavic tribes known as Kievan Rus that originated in the 10th century to the Russian Soviet Federated Socialist Republic of the Soviet Union to present-day Russia. It can be defined as the oral and written literature of the Russian language, one of several Eastern Slavic languages spoken in that region.

Russian culture and literature were influenced by the Eastern Christian culture and civilization, which was centered in Byzantium at Constantinople. The Cyrillic alphabet used in the Russian language was created on the basis of the Greek alphabet. Most of the great Russian literary works have been translated into English. However, the alphabet, a comparatively complicated grammar, different centers of culture, and geographic distance kept Western countries from knowing and enjoying Russia's literature for a long time. The two world wars helped increase international interest in Russian literature.

The most celebrated period of Russian literature was the 19th century, which produced, in a remarkably short period, some of the indisputable masterworks of world literature. It has often been noted that the overwhelming majority of Russian works of world significance were produced within the lifetime of one person, Leo Tolstoy (1828–1910). Indeed, many of them were written within two decades, the 1860s and 1870s, a period

*The great novels of the Russian writer Leo Tolstoy capture the vastness of the Russian landscape and the complexity of its people.*

that perhaps never has been surpassed in any culture for sheer concentrated literary brilliance.

Russian literature, especially of the Imperial and post-Revolutionary periods, has as its defining characteristics an intense concern with philosophical problems, a constant self-consciousness about its relation to the cultures of the West, and a strong tendency toward formal innovation and defiance of received generic norms. The combination of formal radicalism and preoccupation with abstract philosophical issues creates the recognizable aura of Russian classics.

# THE BEGINNINGS OF RUSSIAN LITERATURE

Beginning in ancient times folk poetry flourished among the Eastern Slavs. Written literature started with the introduction of Christianity to Russia in 988. At that time it consisted mainly of historic chronicles, the lives of the saints, and translations from the Greek. The writing and translating were carried on chiefly by monks in monasteries.

The earliest real literary work, a heroic epic, *The Lay of the Host of Igor*, was written in 1187. It deals with the advance of a Russian prince against the Polovtsian army, his imprisonment, escape, and return. It is an interesting bringing together of folk poetry, Byzantine tradition, and the originality of the author. The unknown author was probably a scholar from Kiev, then the cultural center of Russia. In the 13th century Russia was invaded by Tatars, and it took three centuries to shake the Tatars' yoke. No literature could develop under these difficult conditions, but Russian monks kept the literary tradition alive by recording significant events and translating Greek literature.

# CONTACT WITH THE WEST

In the 15th century two major events influenced the direction of the development of Russian literature. The first was the centralization of political and cultural power in the Moscovite state. This resulted in the eventual freeing of Russia from the Tatars. It also resulted in the bringing together of all the literary efforts of all the peoples of the spreading Russian empire into one great literature.

The second event was the invasion of Byzantium by the Turks, which culminated in the fall of Constantinople (the "Second Rome") in 1453. This led the Russians to believe that Moscow was selected by God to be the "Third Rome." This belief has influenced Russian literature for five centuries.

By the 17th century Russia came into closer contact with the West, absorbed Western literary trends, and opened its first theatre. In the 18th century it produced its first great literary figure, Mikhail Lomonosov. Born to simple fisherfolk, Lomonosov became highly educated in almost every field of art and science. In 1755, under his direction, the first Russian university in Moscow was formed. He also worked out a happy combination of the Old Church Slavonic language with the popular spoken tongue of Russia.

Catherine the Great was largely responsible for introducing Western European humanitarian ideas into Russia. These ideas were a powerful influence in the great period of Russian literature that started under Catherine's reign. Denis Fonvizin wrote his famous comedy of manners, *The Minor*, and Ivan Krylov, Russia's La Fontaine, his vivid fables. Aleksandr Radishchev, in *A Journey from Petersburg to Moscow*, sharply criticized corrupt officials.

Gavrila Derzhavin wrote starkly original *Odes*, in which he praises Catherine but satirizes all her entourage. Derzhavin ends this classical period of Russian literature.

## THE 19TH CENTURY

Nikolai Karamzin introduced Romanticism into Russian literature. He also simplified the literary language. His reforms were carried on by Vasily Zhukovsky and produced the pattern for the poetic language of the 19th century. The first quarter of the 19th century was dominated by Romantic poetry. Zhukovsky's 1802 translation of Thomas Gray's *An Elegy Written in a Country Church Yard* ushered in a vogue for the personal, elegiac mode that was soon amplified in the work of Konstantin Batyushkov, Prince Pyotr Vyazemsky, and the young Aleksandr Pushkin. Although there was a call for civic-oriented poetry in the late 1810s and early '20s, most of the strongest poets followed Zhukovsky's lyrical path. However, in the 1820s the mature Pushkin went his own way, producing a series of masterpieces that laid the foundation for his eventual recognition as Russia's national poet (the equivalent of William Shakespeare for English readers or Dante for Italians). Pushkin's works include the Byronic long poems *The Prisoner of the Caucasus* (1820–21) and *The Gypsies* (1824), the novel in verse *Yevgeny Onegin* (published 1833), and the Shakespearean tragedy *Boris Godunov* (1831), as well as exquisite lyrical verse. Pushkin's poetry is remarkable for its classical balance, brilliant and frequently witty use of the Russian literary language, and philosophical content.

During the 1830s a gradual decline in poetry and a rise of prose took place, a shift that coincided with a change in literary institutions. The aristocratic salon, which had been the seedbed for Russian literature, was gradually supplanted by the monthly "thick journals," the editors and critics of which became Russia's tastemakers. The turn to prose was signaled in the work of Pushkin, whose *Tales of the Late Ivan Petrovich Belkin* (1831), *The Queen of Spades* (1834), and *The Captain's Daughter* (1836) all appeared before his death in 1837. Also in the 1830s the first publications

The works of poet, novelist, and dramatist Aleksandr Pushkin express Russian national consciousness, and they are seen as the first works of modern Russian literature.

appeared by Nikolay Gogol, a comic writer of Ukrainian origin, whose grotesquely hilarious oeuvre includes the story *The Nose*, the play *The Government Inspector* (both 1836), and the epic novel *Dead Souls* (1842). Although Gogol was then known primarily as a satirist, he is now appreciated as a verbal magician whose works seem akin to the absurdists of the 20th century. One final burst of poetic energy appeared in the late 1830s in the verse of Mikhail Lermontov, who also wrote *A Hero of Our Time* (1840), the first Russian psychological novel.

In the 1840s the axis of Russian literature shifted decisively from the personal and Romantic to the civic and realistic, a shift presided over by the great Russian literary critic Vissarion Belinsky. Belinsky desired a literature primarily concerned with current social problems, although he never expected it to give up the aesthetic function entirely. By the end of the 1840s, Belinsky's ideas had triumphed. Early works of Russian realism include Ivan Goncharov's antiromantic novel *A Common Story* (1847) and Fyodor Dostoyevsky's *Poor Folk* (1846).

From the 1840s until the turn of the 20th century, the realist novel dominated Russian literature, though it was by no means a monolithic movement. In the early period the favoured method was the "physiological sketch," which often depicted a typical member of the downtrodden classes; quintessential examples are found in Ivan Turgenev's 1852 collection *A Sportsman's Sketches*. In these beautifully crafted stories, Turgenev describes the life of Russian serfs as seen through the eyes of a Turgenev-like narrator; indeed, his powerful artistic depiction was credited with convincing Tsar Alexander II of the need to emancipate the serfs. Turgenev followed *Sketches* with a series of novels, each of which was felt by contemporaries to have captured the essence of Russian society.

The most celebrated is *Fathers and Sons* (1862), in which generational and class conflict in the period of Alexander II's reforms is described through the interactions of the Kirsanov family (father, son, and uncle) with the young "nihilist" Bazarov.

The two other great realists of the 19th century were Dostoyevsky and Leo Tolstoy. Dostoyevsky, who was arrested in 1849 for his involvement in a socialist reading group, reentered the literary scene in the late 1850s. He experienced a religious conversion during his imprisonment, and his novels of the 1860s and '70s are suffused with

*Fyodor Dostoyevsky is one of the world's great novelists. His psychological penetration into the darkest recesses of the human heart exerted a great influence on 20th-century fiction.*

messianic Orthodox ideas. His major novels—*Crime and Punishment* (1866), *The Idiot* (1868–69), *The Possessed* (1872), and *The Brothers Karamazov* (1879–80)—are filled with riveting, often unstable characters and dramatic scenes. While Dostoyevsky delves into the psychology of men and women at the edge, Tolstoy's novels treat the everyday existence of average people. In both *War and Peace* (1865–69) and *Anna Karenina* (1875–77), Tolstoy draws beautifully nuanced portraits filled with deep psychological and sociological insight.

## LEO TOLSTOY

Tolstoy is best known for his two longest works, *War and Peace* (1865–69) and *Anna Karenina* (1875–77), which are commonly regarded as among the finest novels ever written. *War and Peace* in particular seems virtually to define this form for many readers and critics. Among Tolstoy's shorter works, *The Death of Ivan Ilyich* (1886) is usually classed among the best examples of the novella. Especially during his last three decades Tolstoy also achieved world renown as a moral and religious teacher. His doctrine of nonresistance to evil had an important influence on Gandhi. Although Tolstoy's religious ideas no longer command the respect they once did, interest in his life and personality has, if anything, increased over the years.

Most readers will agree with the assessment of the 19th-century British poet and critic Matthew Arnold that a novel by Tolstoy is not a work of art but a piece of life; the Russian author Isaak Babel commented that, if the world could write by itself, it would write like Tolstoy. Critics of diverse schools have agreed that somehow Tolstoy's works seem to elude all artifice. Most have stressed his ability to observe the smallest changes of consciousness and to record the slightest movements of the body. What another novelist would describe as a single act of consciousness, Tolstoy convincingly breaks down into a series of infinitesimally small steps. According to the English writer Virginia Woolf, who took for granted that Tolstoy was "the greatest of all novelists," these observational powers elicited a kind of fear in readers, who "wish to escape from the gaze which Tolstoy fixes on us." Those who visited Tolstoy as an old man also reported feelings of great discomfort when he appeared to understand their unspoken thoughts. It was commonplace to describe him as godlike in his powers and titanic in his struggles to escape the limitations of the human condition. Some viewed Tolstoy as the embodiment of nature and pure vitality, others saw him as the incarnation of the world's conscience, but for almost all who knew him or read his works, he was not just one of the greatest writers who ever lived but a living symbol of the search for life's meaning.

By the early 1880s the hegemony of the realist novel was waning, though what would replace it was unclear. Russian poetry, notwithstanding the civic verse of Nikolay Nekrasov and the subtle lyrics of Afanasy Fet, had not played a central role in the literary process since the 1830s, and drama, despite the able work of Aleksandr Ostrovsky, was a marginal literary activity for most writers. The only major prose writer to appear in the 1880s and '90s was Anton Chekhov, whose specialty was the short story. In his greatest stories—including "The Man in a Case" (1898), "The Lady with a Lapdog" (1899), "The Darling" (1899), and "In the Ravine" (1900)—Chekhov manages to attain all the power of his great predecessors in a remarkably

*Anton Chekhov's stories and plays describe in almost sociological detail the Russian society of his day. However, modern readers value his works chiefly for their deep insight into human emotion.*

compact form. Toward the end of his career, Chekhov also became known for his dramatic work, including such pillars of the world theatrical repertoire as *Uncle Vanya* (1897) and *The Cherry Orchard* (first performed 1904). Chekhov's heirs in the area of short fiction were Maxim Gorky (later the dean of Soviet letters), who began his career by writing sympathetic portraits of various social outcasts, and the aristocrat Ivan Bunin, who emigrated after the Russian Revolution of 1917 and received the Nobel Prize for Literature in 1933.

## THE 20TH CENTURY

The beginning of the 20th century brought with it a new renaissance in Russian poetry and drama, a "Silver Age" that rivaled, and in some respects surpassed, the Pushkinian "Golden Age." The civic orientation that had dominated Russian literature since the 1840s was, for the moment, abandoned. The avant-garde's new cry was "art for art's sake," and the new idols were the French Symbolists. The first, "decadent" generation of Russian Symbolists included the poets Valery Bryusov, Konstantin Balmont, and Zinaida Gippius. The second, more mystically and apocalyptically oriented generation included Aleksandr Blok (perhaps the most talented lyric poet Russia ever produced), the poet and theoretician Vyacheslav Ivanov, and the poet and prose writer Andrey Bely. The Symbolists dominated the literary scene until 1910, when internal dissension led to the movement's collapse.

The period just before and immediately following the Russian Revolution of 1917 was marked by the work of six spectacularly talented, difficult poets. The Futurists Velimir Khlebnikov and Vladimir Mayakovsky engaged in innovative experiments to free poetic discourse from the fetters of tradition. Marina Tsvetayeva, another great poetic experimenter, produced much of her major work outside the country but returned to the Soviet Union in 1939, only to commit suicide there two years later. Boris Pasternak, who won the Nobel Prize for Literature in 1958, produced lyrics of great depth and power in this period, and Osip Mandelshtam created some of the most beautiful and haunting lyric poems in the Russian language.

Anna Akhmatova's brief, finely chiseled lyrics brought her fame at the outset of her career, but later in life she produced such longer works as *Requiem*, written from 1935 to 1940 but published in Russia only in 1989, her

*Anna Akhmatova's principal motif is frustrated and tragic love expressed with an intensely feminine accent and inflection entirely her own.*

memorial to the victims of Joseph Stalin's purges (particularly her son, who was imprisoned in 1937).

Many of the writers who began to publish immediately after the 1917 revolution turned to prose, particularly the short story and the novella. Those who had been inspired by the recent revolution and the subsequent Russian Civil War (1918–20) included Boris Pilnyak (*The Naked Year* [1922]), Isaak Babel (*Red Cavalry* [1926]), and Mikhail Sholokhov, who was awarded the Nobel Prize for Literature in 1965. Others described life in the new Soviet Union with varying degrees of mordant sarcasm; the short stories of Mikhail Zoshchenko, the comic novels of Ilya Ilf and Yevgeny Petrov, and the short novel *Envy* (1927) by Yury Olesha fall into this category. Writing in Russian also flourished in communities of anticommunist exiles in Germany, France, Italy, and the United States, as represented by writers as various as the novelists Vladimir Nabokov and Yevgeny Zamyatin and the theologian-philosophers Vladimir Nikolayevich Lossky, Sergey Bulgakov, and Nikolay Berdyayev.

In the first decade after the revolution, there were also advances in literary theory and criticism, which changed methods of literary study throughout the world. Members of the Moscow Linguistic Circle and of OPOYAZ (Obshchestvo Izucheniya Poeticheskogo Yazyka; Society for the Study of Poetic Language) in Petrograd (now St. Petersburg) combined to create Formalist literary criticism, a movement that concentrated on analyzing the internal structure of literary texts. At the same time, Mikhail Bakhtin began to develop a sophisticated criticism concerned with ethical problems and ways of representing them, especially in the novel, his favourite genre.

By the late 1920s the period of Soviet experimentation had ended. Censorship became much stricter, and many of the best writers were silenced. During the late 1920s and the '30s, there appeared what became known as the classics of Socialist Realism, a literary method that in 1934 was declared to be the only acceptable one for Soviet writers. Only a few of these works produced in this style—notably Fyodor Gladkov's *Cement* (1925), Nikolay Ostrovsky's *How the Steel Was Tempered* (1932–34), and Valentin Katayev's *Time, Forward!* (1932)—have retained some literary interest. The real masterpieces of this period, however, did not fit the canons of Socialist Realism and were not published until many years later. They include Mikhail Bulgakov's grotesquely funny *The Master*

*The favourite subject of Russian novelist and historian Aleksandr Solzhenitsyn, who was exiled from the Soviet Union for some 20 years, was his homeland.*

*and Margarita* (1966–67) and Andrey Platonov's dark pictures of rural and semiurban Russia, *The Foundation Pit* (1973) and *Chevengur* (1972).

With Stalin's death in 1953 and the subsequent "thaw," new writers and trends appeared in the 1950s and early '60s. Vibrant young poets such as Joseph Brodsky, Yevgeny Yevtushenko, and Andrey Voznesensky exerted a significant influence, and Aleksandr Solzhenitsyn emerged from the Soviet prison-camp system (Gulag) and shocked the country and the world with details of his brutal experiences as depicted in *One Day in the Life of Ivan Denisovich* (1962). "Youth" prose on the model of American writer J.D. Salinger's fiction appeared as well, particularly in the work of Vasily Aksyonov and Vladimir Voynovich. By the late 1960s, however, most of these writers had again been silenced. Solzhenitsyn—who was charged with treason shortly after the publication of the first volume of *The*

*Gulag Archipelago* in 1973—and Brodsky, Aksyonov, and Voynovich had all been forced into exile by 1980, and the best writing was again unpublishable.

Practically the only decent writing published from the late 1960s through the early 1980s came from the "village prose" writers, who treated the clash of rural traditions with modern life in a realistic idiom. The most notable members of this group were the novelist Valentin Rasputin and the short-story writer Vasily Shukshin. The morally complex fiction of Yury Trifonov, staged in an urban setting (e.g., *The House on the Embankment* [1976]), stands somewhat apart from the works of Rasputin and Shukshin that praise Russian rural simplicity. Nevertheless, as in the 1930s and '40s, the most important literature of this period was first published outside the Soviet Union. Notable writers included Varlam Shalamov, whose exquisitely artistic stories chronicled the horrors of the prison camps; Andrey Sinyavsky, whose complex novel *Goodnight!* appeared in Europe in 1984, long after he had been forced to leave the Soviet Union; and Venedikt Yerofeyev, whose grotesque latter-day picaresque *Moscow-Petushki*—published in a clandestine (samizdat) edition in 1968—is a minor classic.

Some of the best work published in the 1980s was in poetry, including the work of conceptualists such as Dmitry Prigov and the meta-metaphoric poetry of Aleksey Parshchikov, Olga Sedakova, Ilya Kutik, and others. The turbulent 1990s were a difficult period for most Russian writers and poets. The publishing industry, adversely affected by the economic downturn, struggled to regain its footing in the conditions of a market economy. Nonetheless, private foundations began awarding annual literary prizes, such as the Russian Booker Prize and the Little Booker Prize. The so-called Anti-Booker Prize—its name, a protest against the British origins of the Booker Prize, was selected to emphasize that it was a Russian award for Russian writers—was first presented in 1995 by the *Nezavisimaya Gazeta*. Tatyana Tolstaya began to occupy a prominent role following the publication of her novel *The Slynx* (2000), a satire about a disastrous hypothetical future for Moscow. Some critics considered the decade the "twilight period in Russian literature," because of the departure from traditional psychological novels about contemporary life in favour of detective novels. Indeed, such novels were among the best-selling fiction of the period, particularly the work of Boris Akunin, whose *Koronatsiia* ("Coronation") won the Anti-Booker Prize in 2000.

Almost no one expected the Soviet Union to come suddenly to an end. The effects of this event on literature have been enormous. The period of *glasnost* under Gorbachev and the subsequent collapse of the U.S.S.R. led first to a dramatic easing and then to the abolition of censorship. Citizenship was restored to émigré writers, and Solzhenitsyn returned to Russia. *Doctor Zhivago* and *We* were published in Russia, as were the works of Nabokov, Solzhenitsyn, Voynovich, and many others. The divisions between Soviet and émigré and between official and unofficial literature came to an end. Russians experienced the heady feeling that came with absorbing, at great speed, large parts of their literary tradition that had been suppressed and with having free access to Western literary movements. A Russian form of postmodernism, fascinated with a pastiche of citations, arose, along with various forms of radical experimentalism. During this period, readers and writers sought to understand the past, both literary and historical, and to comprehend the chaotic, threatening, and very different present.

# CONCLUSION

Russia's culture continues to be vibrant and its writers, artists, architects, performers, and directors continue to produce interesting work. Poetry, novels, criticism, and other nonfiction all remain important in the literary milieu, which continues to be lively, even to the point of contentiousness. The Russian tradition of excellence in dance and classical music continues, while the feminist protests of Pussy Riot became a cause célèbre for some in the West.

However, Russian society—although more stable than it was in the 1990s—became less free and less democratic under Vladimir Putin. In August 2014, a new law imposing restrictions on users of social media entered into effect in Russia. This required bloggers with more than 3,000 daily readers to register with Russia's official mass-media regulator, Roskomnadzor, and to conform to regulations governing the country's larger media outlets. It included measures to ensure that bloggers could not remain anonymous and mandated that social networks maintain six months of data on users. It also required internet companies to allow the authorities access to users' information, which had to be stored on servers based in Russian territory.

Governmental interference is hardly a new theme in Russian culture, though. In fact, literature and the arts in Russia have flourished in the face of censorship for centuries and there is no reason to believe that will change any time soon.

**AUTOCRACY** A government in which one person has unlimited power.

**AUTONOMY** The power or right of self-government.

**CANTATA** A poem, story, or play set to music to be sung by a chorus and soloists.

**COMPULSORY** Required by or as if by law.

**CONSTRUCTIVISM** A Russian artistic and architectural movement that was first influenced by Cubism and Futurism and is generally considered to have been initiated in 1913 with the "painting reliefs"—abstract geometric constructions—of Vladimir Tatlin.

**DIKTAT** A harsh settlement unilaterally imposed.

**FORMALISM** An innovative 20th-century Russian school of literary criticism that stressed the importance of form and technique over content and looked for the specificity of literature as an autonomous verbal art.

**FRESCO** A method of painting water-based pigments on freshly applied plaster, usually on wall surfaces.

*GLASNOST* (Russian: "openness") The Soviet policy of open discussion of political and social issues.

**HAGIOGRAPHY** The body of literature describing the lives and veneration of the Christian saints.

**HEGEMONY** The social, cultural, ideological, or economic influence exerted by a dominant group.

**HIERATIC** Highly stylized or formal.

**ICON** A representation of sacred personages or events in mural painting, mosaic, or wood.

**ICONOGRAPHY** The traditional or conventional images or symbols associated with a subject and especially a religious or legendary subject.

**LIBRETTO** The text of an opera or musical.

**METRE** The rhythmic pattern of a poetic line. Various principles, based on the natural rhythms of language, have been devised to organize poetic lines into rhythmic units.

**PATRIARCH** The head of one of various Eastern churches, such as the Russian Orthodox Church.

**PICARESQUE** Of, relating to, suggesting, or being a type of fiction dealing with the adventures of a usually mischievous or dishonest character.

**PRIMITIVISM** An artistic movement that sought to create art that was like that of peoples the artists considered more closely tied to nature and less shaped by society.

**PROPAGANDA** The dissemination of information— facts, arguments, rumours, half-truths, or lies—to influence public opinion.

**REPERTOIRE** A list or supply of dramas, operas, pieces, or parts that a company or person is prepared to perform.

**ROMANTICISM** A late 18th- and early 19th-century literary and artistic movement marked chiefly by an emphasis on the imagination and emotions.

**SALON** A fashionable assemblage of notables (such as literary figures, artists, or statesmen) held by custom at the home of a prominent person.

**SECULAR** Not religious or related to religion.

**SUPREMATISM** The first movement of pure geometrical abstraction in painting, originated by Kazimir Malevich in Russia in about 1913.

**SYMBOLISM** A loosely organized literary and artistic movement that originated with a group of French poets in the late 19th century. Symbolist artists sought to express individual emotional experience through the subtle and suggestive use of highly symbolized language.

# BIBLIOGRAPHY

An excellent survey of Soviet culture as a whole is Andrei Sinyavsky (Andrei Siniavskii), *Soviet Civilization: A Cultural History*, trans. from Russian by Joanne Turnbull (1990).

Ethnicity is the focus of Robert J. Kaiser, *The Geography of Nationalism in Russia and the USSR* (1994); Jeff Chinn and Robert J. Kaiser, *Russians as the New Minority: Ethnicity and Nationalism in the Soviet Successor States* (1996); and Michael Rywkin, *Moscow's Lost Empire* (1994).

The ethnic and religious composition of the population and its implications are discussed in David C. Lewis, *After Atheism: Religion and Ethnicity in Russia and Central Asia* (2000); Christopher Williams and Thanasis D. Sfikas, *Ethnicity and Nationalism in Russia, the CIS, and the Baltic States* (1999); Gail Fondahl, *Gaining Ground?: Evenkis, Land, and Reform in Southeastern Siberia* (1998); Viktor Kozlov, *The Peoples of the Soviet Union*, trans. by Pauline M. Tiffen (1988; originally published in Russian, 1975); Ludmilla Alexeyeva, *Soviet Dissent: Contemporary Movements for National, Religious, and Human Rights*, trans. by Carol Pearce and John Glad (1987); Ronald Wixman, *The Peoples of the USSR: An Ethnographic Handbook* (1984, reissued 1988); Hedrick Smith, *The Russians* (1976, reissued 1985); Farley Mowat, *The Siberians* (1970, reissued 1982; also published as *Sibir: My Discovery of Siberia*, 1970); and M.G. Levin and L.P. Potapov (eds.), *The Peoples of Siberia* (1964; originally published in Russian, 1956). Valuable additional material on many aspects of the Russian republic and its peoples is found in Archie Brown, Michael Kaser, and Gerald S. Smith (eds.), *The Cambridge Encyclopedia of Russia and the Former Soviet Union*, 2nd ed. (1994); and Stephen White (ed.), *Political and Economic Encyclopaedia of the Soviet Union and Eastern Europe* (1990).

An excellent general history of Russian literature is Victor Terras, *A History of Russian Literature* (1991). Outstanding books on the interaction of literature and society include, for the 19th century, Isaiah Berlin, *Russian Thinkers*, ed. by Henry Hardy and Aileen Kelly (1978, reissued 1994); and, for the Soviet period, Ronald Hingley, *Russian Writers and Soviet Society, 1917–1978* (1979, reissued 1981).

Important books on Russian art include Camilla Gray, *The Great Experiment: Russian Art, 1863–1922* (1962, reissued as *The Russian Experiment in Art, 1863–1922*, 1971); Angelica Zander Rudenstine (ed.), *Russian Avant-Garde Art: The George Costakis Collection* (1981). G.H. Hamilton, *The Art and Architecture of Russia*, 3rd ed. (1983), is a survey of all the arts of Russia. *All the Empty Palaces: The Merchant Patrons of Modern Art in Pre-Revolutionary Russia* (1983), is an original study of important developments in the history of European art

Hubert Faensen, Vladimir Ivanov, and Klaus G. Beyer, *Early Russian Architecture* (1975; originally published in German, 1972), is a useful introduction. M. Il'ina and A. Aleksandrova, *Moscow Monuments of Architecture, 18th–the First Third of the Nineteenth Century*, 2 vol. (1975) and E. Kirichenko, *Moscow Architectural Monuments of the 1830–1910s* (1977) both feature parallel English and Russian texts.

Konstantin Rudnitsky (Konstantin Rudnitskii), *Russian and Soviet Theater, 1905–1932*, trans. from Russian by Roxane Permar, ed. by Lesley Milne (1988), a copiously illustrated work, provides a good introduction to the golden age of Russian theatre. Jay Leyda, *Kino: A History of the Russian and Soviet Film*, 3rd ed. (1983), is an authoritative study of developments since tsarist times. Essential and classic texts concerned with the nature of film include Sergei Eisenstein, *The Film Sense* (1947), and *Film Form* (1949), two essays in film theory, translated from Russian and available in various later editions of the author's theoretical essays.

# INDEX